English Skills

Published by Collins
An imprint of HarperCollins*Publishers*
77–85 Fulham Palace Road
Hammersmith
London
W6 8JB

Browse the complete Collins catalogue at
www.collinseducation.com

© HarperCollins*Publishers* Limited 2011, on behalf of the author

First published in 2006 by Folens Limited.

ISBN-13: 978-0-00-743721-4

All rights reserved. No part of this publication may be reproduced, stored in a retrieval system, or transmitted in any form or by any means, electronic, mechanical, photocopying, recording or otherwise, without the prior written permission of the Publisher or a licence permitting restricted copying in the United Kingdom issued by the Copyright Licensing Agency Ltd, 90 Tottenham Court Road, London W1T 4LP.

British Library Cataloguing in Publication Data
A catalogue record for this publication is available from the British Library.

Every effort has been made to trace copyright holders and to obtain their permission for the use of copyright material. The authors and publishers will gladly receive any information enabling them to rectify any error or omission in subsequent editions.

Editor: Geraldine Sowerby
Layout artist: Patricia Hollingsworth
Illustrations: Tony Randell
Cover design: Martin Cross
Editorial consultant: Helen Whittaker

Printed and bound by L.EG.O S.p.A. - Lavis (Trento)

Contents

Reading	The Fox and the Woodcutter	4
Activities		5
Phonics	Three-syllable Words	6
Grammar	Capital Letters and Full Stops	7
Writing	Profile	8
Language	Using Words	9
Reading	Echo	10
Activities		11
Phonics	Four-syllable Words	12
Grammar	Capital Letters	13
Writing	Addressing an Envelope	14
Language	Using Words	15
Reading	Tutankhamun's Tomb	16
Activities		17
Phonics	Word Endings: 'ild' and 'ind'	18
Grammar	Capital Letters	19
Writing		20
Language	Using Words	21
Reading	The Great White Shark	22
Activities		23
Phonics	Fun Time	24
Grammar	Revision	25
Writing		26
Language	Using Words	27
Reading	The Hummingbird	28
Activities		29
Phonics	Word Endings: 'ar' and 'er'	30
Grammar	Adjectives	31
Writing		32
Language	Using Words	33
Reading	The Match Girl	34
Activities		35
Phonics		36
Grammar	Singular and Plural	37
Writing		38
Language	Using Words	39
Reading	Boeing 747	40
Activities		41
Phonics	Word Endings: 'or', 'ur' and 'ir'	42
Grammar	Masculine and Feminine	43
Writing	Proofreading	44
Language	Using Words	45
Reading	One Man's Horse	46
Activities		47
Phonics	G or J?	48
Grammar	Nouns	49

Writing		50
Language	Using Words	51
Reading	The Polar Bear	52
Activities		53
Phonics	Silent Letters: 'g' and 't'	54
Grammar	Nouns	55
Writing		56
Language	Using Words	57
Reading	Walk on the Moon	58
Activities		59
Phonics	Silent Letters: 'b' and 'l'	60
Grammar	Adjectives	61
Language	Using Words	62
Language	Using Words	63
Reading	Planet Problem!	64
Activities		65
Language	Fun Time	66
Grammar	Homonyms	67
Writing		68
Grammar	Verbs	69
Reading	Tyrannosaurus	70
Activities		71
Phonics	Three-letter Blends	72
Grammar	Quotation Marks	73
Writing	Descriptive	74
Language	Using Words	75
Reading	Dako	76
Activities		77
Language	Fun Time	78
Grammar	Suffixes	79
Writing		80
Language	Using Words	81
Reading	The Marrog	82
Activities		83
Grammar	Adverbs	84
Writing	Adjectives	85
Language	Using Words	86
Language	Fun Time	87
Reading	Everest	88
Activities		89
Phonics	Three-letter Blends: 'shr' and 'thr'	90
Grammar	Verbs	91
Writing		92
Phonics	Revision	93
Language		94
Activities		95
Grammar		96

Reading

 A Read the story.

The Fox and the Woodcutter

A fox that was being chased by huntsmen begged a woodcutter to *shelter* him. The woodcutter *directed* him into his cottage, and when the huntsmen arrived they asked the woodcutter if a fox had *chanced* that way.

"I saw no fox today," said the woodcutter, but he pointed at the same time with his finger to the spot where the fox was hiding. The huntsmen did not take the *hint*. However, the fox saw what the woodcutter did as he was looking out through a crack in the cottage door.

When the fox-hunters had gone away, the fox stole quietly out into the open, and was about to clear off without a word to the woodcutter. "You *ungrateful* beast," said the man angrily. "You were about to leave without a word of thanks! Have you no manners?"

The fox paused and then said: "If you had been as honest with your finger as you were with your tongue, I should not have gone without *bidding* you goodbye!" And off he trotted towards his den.

Activities

A **Answer these questions.**

1. What is the name of the story?
2. Who was chasing the fox?
3. What did the huntsmen ask the woodcutter?
4. How did the woodcutter let them know where the fox was hiding?
5. Why did the huntsmen not discover the fox?
6. How did the fox see what the woodcutter was doing?
7. Why was the fox leaving without thanking the woodcutter?
8. What did the fox say to the woodcutter?

B **Look up the words in *italics* in your dictionary. Write a sentence for each one.**

C **Summarise the story in your own words. Use about ten sentences.**

D **Name the animal described in each clue.**

1. I butt and push people with my horns. _____
2. I live at the seaside and I have pincers. _____
3. I swoop and snatch my prey with my talons. _____
4. I have wings and I sleep upside down. _____
5. I have antlers and my young are called fawns. _____
6. I use my prickly spines to defend myself. _____
7. I float in the sea and sting you. _____
8. I am a member of the weasel family and I live in a sett. _____

E **You are the fox looking through the crack in the cottage door. Describe and draw what you see.**

Phonics

Three-syllable Words

A Divide each word into three syllables.

1. how/ev/er
2. difficult
3. different
4. memory
5. hospital
6. magician
7. lullaby
8. labrador
9. magazine
10. professor
11. mystery
12. gallery
13. direction
14. computer
15. reflection
16. editor

B Join the syllables. Write the words.

1. el — y — tric _____
2. gen — er — al _____
3. lad — ec — bird _____
4. pot — at — o _____
5. ratt — le — snake _____
6. whis — a — la _____
7. trop — a — way _____
8. um — brel — bout _____
9. stow — ic — al _____
10. round — per — ing _____

C Make a new word from each three-syllable word below.

1. telescope _____
2. yesterday _____
3. unlucky _____
4. suddenly _____
5. restaurant _____
6. tomorrow _____
7. wonderful _____
8. volunteer _____
9. trampoline _____
10. underground _____

D Unscramble the letters to make three-syllable words.

1. fericon _____
2. bllabastek _____
3. wichassnde _____
4. laderamma _____
5. urrichane _____
6. onlemdae _____

Grammar

Capital Letters and Full Stops

> Always end a sentence with a full stop.

 A Rewrite this paragraph using full stops.

I've written this message in the sand with a very long stick You might wonder why I wrote with a long stick You might also wonder why you're sinking Well I can tell you I wrote with a long stick because the sand you're sinking in is actually quicksand Thanks for reading my message I hope you enjoyed it

B Rewrite these sentences using capital letters and full stops.

1. my friend has a bow and arrow
2. we saw a cowboy film
3. the chief smoked a peace pipe
4. she lived with her husband in a large wigwam
5. all the young braves danced around the campfire
6. they traded their guns for buffalo hides
7. a pony galloped into the army fort
8. there was a young warrior behind the rock

 C There are two sentences in each of the following. Rewrite them using capital letters and full stops.

1. femi called with her friend yasmin today i showed them my new pet rabbit
2. we had to stay inside all day i was delighted when the rain stopped
3. the outlaws stopped the coach and robbed the passengers everybody was terrified
4. the wolf called the frog and the bear they promised to help him
5. the shepherd watched over his flock the wolf did not dare come near
6. the rocket lifted off it was going on a long voyage into outer space
7. she worked long hours on the farm she had the finest herd of cattle in the land
8. a huge pirate stood on the deck his name was blackbeard
9. snow fell during the night when i awoke, i wanted to make a snowman
10. the summer morning was bright and fine we set out for the seaside

Writing

Profile

A Fill in the words.

My name is _____ and I am _____ years old.
I live at _____ .
I have _____ hair and _____ eyes.
I am _____ tall and weigh _____ kilograms.
There are _____ in my family.
Their names are _____ .
The youngest in the family is _____ .
I attend _____ .
My teacher's name is _____ .

B Write three sentences for each of these topics.

1. My best friend.
   _____
   _____
   _____

2. My favourite food.
   _____
   _____
   _____

3. My favourite TV programmes.
   _____
   _____
   _____

4. My favourite games.
   _____
   _____
   _____

C Describe your neighbourhood under these headings.

1. Its location, whether in the city, town or country.
2. Interesting facts you know about your area.
3. Where you shop.
4. Neighbours.
5. People who work in your area.

Using Words

Language

A Choose the correct word.

1. A lion has four _____. (hooves, tusks, paws)
2. A lion _____. (barks, roars, bellows)
3. A lioness has no _____. (tail, mane, claws)
4. A lion is smaller than an _____. (ant, elephant, otter)
5. A young lion is called a _____. (puppy, kitten, cub)
6. A lion cannot _____. (swim, leap, fly)
7. A lion lives in a _____. (coop, hole, den)
8. A lion has a covering of _____. (skin, wool, spines)

B Choose the correct word.

| mane | hooves | stable | hair | hay |
| tail | stallion | neighs | mare | foal |

A horse has four _____ , a long _____ and a _____ growing on its neck. It has a coat of _____ . A horse eats _____ and lives in a _____ . A young horse is called a _____ . A female horse is called a _____ and a male horse is called a _____ . A horse _____ to make itself heard.

C Choose the correct word.

1. A swan has a coat of white _____. (hair, feathers, skin)
2. A swan has two _____. (tails, necks, wings)
3. A swan's beak is _____. (blue, red, yellow)
4. A swan _____. (croaks, hisses, barks)
5. A swan is a graceful _____. (fish, horse, bird)
6. A swan has a long _____. (tail, neck, ear)
7. A swan has webbed _____. (wings, beak, feet)
8. A swan cannot _____. (fly, swim, talk)

9

Reading

 A Read the story.

Echo

Echo was one of the many Greek *goddesses*, but she had one great *fault*. She talked too much. One day, she spoke rather rudely to the great god Juno, and he was so angry that he *forbade* her to use her voice again. She would only be able to repeat what she heard, he told her. However since she was so fond of having the last word, she could only repeat the last words of others.

Echo felt that she was now a sort of parrot. She was ashamed and hid in the forest.

A youth named Narcissus used to hunt in the forest. One day, he became separated from his friends, and Echo saw him. She crept closer, but Narcissus heard her rustling among the bushes, and wondered who was hiding in the *undergrowth*.

"Who is here?" he called out.

"Here!" answered Echo.

"Here I am. Come!" shouted Narcissus.

"I am come," answered Echo, and appeared from the trees.

When Narcissus saw a stranger, however, he turned and walked slowly away, leaving Echo sad and lonely.

After this, Echo never again showed herself. She faded away until only her voice was left.

Her voice has been heard for many, many years, in forests, near mountains and cliffs and caves. She *mimics* the cries of seagulls and mocks the barking of dogs. But she always sounds sad and *mournful*, and makes lonely places seem more lonely still as she repeats a caller's last words.

Activities

A **Answer these questions.**

1. What was Echo's one great fault? _____.
2. Why was Juno angry with Echo? _____.
3. Why was Echo ashamed? _____.
4. What did Narcissus do in the forest? _____.
5. Why did Narcissus walk slowly away? _____.
6. When Echo faded away, what was left of her? _____.
7. Where has Echo's voice been heard? _____.
8. How does Echo sound? _____.

B **Look up the words in *italics* in your dictionary. Write a sentence for each one.**

C **Summarise the story in your own words. Use about ten sentences.**

D **The word Echo is used in radio communication as a code word for the letter E. Unscramble the letters to find out the other words in this alphabet and complete the chart.**

phaal	A _____		nobervem	N _____
avbro	B _____		caros	O _____
cliehar	C _____		appa	P _____
tadel	D _____		becque	Q _____
cheo	E _____		eorom	R _____
ftrotox	F _____		siearr	S _____
lfgo	G _____		gotan	T _____
helot	H _____		unirmfo	U _____
diain	I _____		torvic	V _____
etjuli	J _____		wkeyhis	W _____
loki	K _____		rayx	X _____
mali	L _____		keeyan	Y _____
kmie	M _____		luzu	Z _____

11

Phonics

Four-syllable Words

 A **Divide each word into four syllables. Match the word to its meaning.**

1. su/per/mar/ket   a shape with two halves that are exactly the same
2. symmetrical   someone who doesn't eat meat or fish
3. vegetarian   large, green fruit
4. watermelon   a thousand years
5. television   a large shop where you pay for your goods as you leave
6. millennium   equipment that shows moving pictures and sound
7. conversation   surroundings
8. environment   talking between two or more people

B **Join the syllables. Write the words.**

1. rid   cov   ul   tion   _____
2. in   ic   a   y   _____
3. dis   vit   er   le   _____
4. imp   pop   ib   tion   _____
5. in   for   ma   ous   <u>ridiculous</u>
6. un   oss   u   lar   _____

 C **Rearrange the syllables to make a word.**

1. gent in i tell _____
2. a gla tor di _____
3. ci ous du de _____
4. con tu gra late _____
2. mat e ics math _____
3. cal la tor cu _____

 D **Make a new word from each four-syllable word below. You do not need to use all of the letters.**

1. concentrated _____
2. tarantula _____
3. dictionary _____
4. Tutenkhamun _____
5. concentration _____
6. California _____
7. contradiction _____
8. balaclava _____
9. sentimental _____
10. communicate _____

12

Grammar

Capital Letters

> **Capital letters are used for:**
> a) The beginning of a sentence – **M**y teacher is very intelligent.
> b) 'I' when used on its own – **I** was sick, so **I** went to bed.
> c) People's names – **J**ames and **J**ohn **W**hite are twins.

A Rewrite these sentences using capital letters.

1. at the end of every sentence there is a full stop.
2. my father spoke to doctor smith about my sore throat.
3. meera patel was absent from school yesterday.
4. i have a baby sister named jane.
5. pears and apples are delicious fruit.
6. peter and i went to the pictures together.
7. larry daly and michael rice are cousins.
8. erina and hana were at the circus.
9. every day the teacher gives us homework.
10. may i help you paint the picture?

> **Capital letters are used for:**
> a) The names of days – **S**unday, **M**onday.
> b) The names of the months – **A**pril, **F**ebruary.
> c) The names of special days and festivals – **C**hristmas **D**ay.

B Rewrite these sentences using capital letters.

1. Last tuesday the school team won the football final.
2. We have no school on friday.
3. People all over the world celebrate christmas day.
4. November comes between october and december.
5. Muriel's mother made pancakes on shrove tuesday.
6. Peter's best friend was born on new year's day.
7. We went to the seaside for the easter weekend.
8. In the united states of america, the fourth of july is called independence day.
9. April the first is called april fool's day.
10. The school holidays lasted from july to september.

13

Writing

Addressing an Envelope

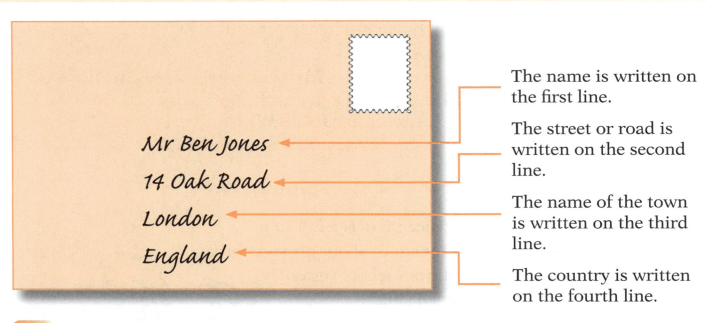

A Write the word that each abbreviation stands for.

1. Rd _____
2. St _____
3. Dr _____
4. Ave _____
5. Sq _____

6. Tce _____
7. Pk _____
8. Gdns _____
9. Gro _____
10. Cres _____

B Write your name and address on an envelope.

Using Words

Language

  A **Write the correct words.**

> gobbles and struts   quacks and waddles   caws and flaps her wings
> hoots and flits   sings and soars   cackles and struts   coos and flutters

1. The eagle __screams__ and __swoops__.
2. The owl _____ and _____.
3. The turkey _____ and _____.
4. The crow _____ and _____.
5. The pigeon _____ and _____.
6. The duck _____ and _____.
7. The lark _____ and _____.
8. The hen _____ and _____.

  B **Write the correct words.**

> bleats and frisks   purrs and slinks   barks and runs   brays and trots
> roars and prowls   howls and lopes   chatters and climbs

1. The horse __neighs__ and __gallops__.
2. The dog _____ and _____.
3. The wolf _____ and _____.
4. The donkey _____ and _____.
5. The cat _____ and _____.
6. The lion _____ and _____.
7. The monkey _____ and _____.
8. The lamb _____ and _____.

C **Write the correct words.**

> hoot   twang   rumble   tick   jingle   beat   screech   crack

1. The _____ of a drum.
2. The _____ of a train.
3. The _____ of a horn.
4. The _____ of a clock.
5. The _____ of brakes.
6. The _____ of a bow.
7. The _____ of a whip.
8. The _____ of coins.

15

Reading

 A Read the text.

Tutankhamun's Tomb

Tutankhamun was king of Egypt nearly four and a half thousand years ago. He was Pharaoh from the age of about nine until his death, ten years later.

In 1922, the British *archaeologist*, Howard Carter, found Tutankhamun's tomb in Egypt's Valley of the Kings, after a search lasting nearly six years. Its entrance had been hidden by loose earth caused by digging at another tomb nearby.

The ancient Egyptians believed in a life after death, which they called the afterlife. So that they could enjoy it properly, their bodies were *preserved* and their possessions were buried with them so they would be able to carry on using them in the afterlife.

Tutankhamun's tomb contained more than 5,000 objects, many of which were covered in gold. There was beautiful furniture, clothing and jewellery. Carter also found chariots, weapons and armour, as well as statues of gods and animals, model ships, toys and games. A lifelike gold mask covered the head and shoulders of Tutankhamun's *mummy*.

There are a couple of strange stories surrounding Tutankhamun. For many years, there were rumours of a 'mummy's curse'. People who believed in the curse said that everyone who entered Tutankhamun's tomb was *doomed* to an early death. In fact, members of the expedition who entered the tomb didn't die any younger than those who didn't.

Another mystery was how Tutankhamun himself died. For some time, archaeologists thought he might have been murdered, but recent scans of his mummy show that he actually died of an *infection* after breaking his leg.

16

Activities

A **Answer these questions.**

1. Who was Tutankhamun?
2. What happened in 1922?
3. Why was Tutankhamun's tomb difficult to find?
4. Why were ancient Egyptians buried with their possessions?
5. Explain the rumour of the 'mummy's curse'.
6. What evidence shows that the 'mummy's curse' didn't really exist?
7. How did archaeologists used to think Tutankhamun might have died?
8. How did Tutankhamun actually die?

B **Look up the words in *italics* in your dictionary. Write a sentence for each one.**

C **Summarise the story in your own words. Use about ten sentences.**

D **Change the verbs in brackets into the past tense.**

"Today is the day!" thought Diarmuid as he got ready for his entrance test to become a Fianna warrior. He (feel) _____ a bit nervous as he (do) _____ up his bootlaces. He (eat) _____ some breakfast to give him strength and he (fly) _____ out the door to the test. Diarmuid was tested on everything: he (fight) _____ off nine warriors while standing in a hole; he (write) _____ out all the ancient stories perfectly; he (swim) _____ against a raging current; and he ran so fast and so deftly that not a leaf (shake) _____ around him. When the bell (ring) _____ at the end of the test, he was told that he had been accepted into the Fianna. He (tear) _____ off his armour and (sing) _____ and danced all the way home.

E **You are a warrior who is training to join the Fianna. Describe your training programme.**

Phonics

Word Endings: 'ild' and 'ind'

A **Join the ild words to their meaning.**

1. child   gentle and good-tempered
2. mild   excited or out of control
3. wild   a young boy or girl

B **Choose the correct ind word.**

1. We should always be _____ (kind, find) to animals.
2. Mansa helped the _____ (grind, blind) woman to find her key.
3. Millers _____ (mind, grind) wheat to make flour.
4. I had to _____ (wind, mind) my baby sister.
5. The doctor had to _____ (bind, find) the cut with a bandage.
6. Abdul tried to _____ (kind, wind) the clockwork car.

C **Write the ind word which matches each clue.**

1. Unable to see   _ _ _ _ d.
2. Discover   _ _ _ d.
3. Crush into small pieces   _ _ _ _ d.
4. Treats others well   _ _ _ d.
5. Wrap up tightly   _ _ _ d.
6. Moving air   _ _ _ d.

D **Write ild or ind to finish the poem.**

"I have two guardian angels,"
said the little ch _ _ _ .
"One is wildly wicked
and the other's meek and m _ _ _ .
And when I misbehave
or when I am unk _ _ _ ,
The mild one's very sorry
But the w _ _ _ one's hard to f _ _ _ !"

Grammar

Capital Letters

Capital letters are used for:
a) The names of places – Italy, Spain.
b) Words formed from the names of places – Brazilian, Bengali.
c) A person's nationality – Samoan, Dutch.

 A Rewrite these sentences using capital letters.

1. my pen friend collects irish stamps.
2. many norwegian fishing trawlers fish off the coasts of canada and greenland.
3. the italian singer sang at the music festival in cambridge.
4. frederick chopin, a polish composer, was born near warsaw.
5. in the new supermarket you can buy french wine and dutch cheese.
6. the kenyan team will play south africa in johannesburg on saturday.
7. last february i received a letter from my pen pal in india.
8. ben lee bought a swiss watch on friday.

 B Write the the nationality of the people from these place names.

England ___English___   Vietnam _____
Australia _____   Pakistan _____
Germany _____   Russia _____
Holland _____   India _____
Ireland _____   Argentina _____
Namibia _____   Spain _____
France _____   Sweden _____

C Complete the chart with other words that use capital letters.

Names of people	Names of places	Days, months	Brand names	Initials
Rashid Prasad	London	Wednesday	Coca Cola	WHO
Anna Yung	Egypt	July	Sony	USA

Writing

A Rewrite this paragraph.
Use words from the list to replace **nice**.

| local | friendly | enormous | gorgeous | delicious | mouth-watering |
| wooden | hand-carved | impatient | thatched | expensive |

One day the nice giant decided to visit our school. We thought it was very nice of him. It was a nice day. We were so busy that we never even heard the poor giant knocking on our nice door. Before we knew what had happened that nice giant had lifted our nice roof to see if we were inside.

B The giant became angry when a class bully called him ugly. Write what happened next.

C 1. Make a list of all the good things about being a giant. Then make a list of all the bad things. Which list is the longest?

Good things	Bad things
1. I can see over heads at concerts!	1.
2.	2.
3.	3.
4.	4.
5.	5.

2. What do you think a giant would eat? What would he have for breakfast? Dinner? Tea?

Language

Using Words

A   Copy and complete. Write **has** or **have**.

1. The pups _____ meat for dinner but the cat _____ fish.
2. We _____ to meet the lady who _____ the books.
3. A whale _____ lungs but a fish _____ gills.
4. The girls _____ measles and the boys _____ the mumps.
5. The soldiers _____ guns and their captains _____ swords.
6. _____ you heard the orders he _____ given us?
7. _____ she seen the present you _____ bought?
8. A weightlifter _____ to _____ very strong arms.
9. I _____ a funny joke to tell you!
10. That joke _____ to be the worst I _____ ever heard!

B   Copy and complete. Write **did** or **done**.

1. Where _____ you leave your money?
2. She _____ not know if he had _____ his chores.
3. Dad _____ the cooking while Mum _____ her painting.
4. What have you _____ with my pencil?
5. I've _____ all I'm going to do.
6. Alice _____ very well in her tests.
7. _____ it happen on Tuesday or Wednesday?
8. I _____ my homework as soon as I got home from school.
9. _____ a famous artist paint it or was it _____ by an art student?
10. I _____ not want to know how the magician _____ the trick.

C   Write **did, done, has** or **have**.

I _____ just arrived home from school and I _____ loads of homework that _____ to be _____ before I can meet my friends. If I _____ my homework _____ before four o'clock, then I can _____ my friends over. They _____ loads of homework to do too unless they _____ it already.

Reading

A Read the text.

The Great White Shark

The great white shark is one of the largest sharks in the world. Adult males usually grow to about four metres long, although they can sometimes reach six metres. Great white sharks are found in warm ocean waters across the world, and they are equally at home hunting close to shore and in deep water.

Great white sharks are *efficient* hunters. They have a very good sense of smell, sharp eyesight, and can swim at speeds of up to forty-five kilometres per hour; they use all these abilities to track down their prey.

Great white sharks hunt fish, sea lions, seals, sea-birds, rays, small whales, turtles, porpoises and even other sharks. They attack from below, their grey backs offering good *camouflage* against the water when seen from above. Great whites have huge, powerful mouths, with up to three thousand sharp, triangular, *serrated* teeth. When a great white shark catches up with its prey, it takes a single, large bite and waits for its victim to become weak from blood loss, before closing in for the kill.

Great whites have a *reputation* as man-eaters, and although they are not as much of a danger as some people claim, they do attack between five and ten people each year. Experts think these attacks happen when sharks mistake humans for seals. When sharks attack people, they tend to take a single bite and then swim away. People who have died from shark attacks have died from losing a lot of blood; not from being eaten.

Although great white sharks are found in many different areas around the world, their numbers have been *decreasing* and they are now *endangered*. This is mainly because fishermen hunt them for their jaws, teeth, and fins, and also for sport. In an effort to prevent the great white shark from becoming *extinct*, laws have been passed in many countries to protect it.

Activities

A **Answer these questions.**

1. What is special about the great white shark?

2. Where do great white sharks live?

3. Name one ability a great white shark uses to track down its prey.

4. Why is the great white shark's grey back useful?

5. Why do experts think great white sharks attack humans?

6. Do sharks eat people?

7. Why are great white sharks endangered?

8. What do you think the laws protecting the great white shark might say?

B **Look up the words in *italics* in your dictionary. Write a sentence for each one.**

C **Summarise the story in your own words. Use about ten sentences.**

Phonics

Fun Time

A **Write the words. They all begin with the letter c.**

1. A large country in North America. _____
2. This is a prickly plant. _____
3. He/she carries clubs for a golfer. _____
4. A floor covering. _____
5. It tells the days and months of the year. _____
6. It is a boat without a keel, pointed at both ends. _____
7. These keep the light out of a room. _____
8. He/she is given authority over a group or team. _____
9. A prisoner is kept in this very small room. _____
10. It is a compartment for the pilot of an aircraft. _____
11. They are edible grains. _____
12. A bright yellow bird like a budgie. _____
13. A knitted woollen jacket. _____
14. Films are shown in these. _____
15. She was a famous queen of ancient Egypt. _____

B **Unscramble these days, seasons and months. Find them in the wordsearch.**

Sadaytur _____
bervemNo _____
intWer _____
eptSberem _____
ngriSp _____
daynMo _____
tuAumn _____
Weddaynes _____
stguAu _____
uaSynd _____
Fruaebry _____
Surmme _____

S	E	P	T	E	M	B	W	L	W
A	S	U	N	D	A	Y	I	I	E
Y	A	E	S	A	T	N	N	M	D
R	T	A	P	U	L	O	T	O	N
A	U	A	R	T	R	V	E	N	E
U	R	U	I	U	E	E	R	D	S
R	D	G	N	M	I	M	N	A	D
B	A	U	G	N	D	B	B	Y	A
E	Y	S	U	M	M	E	R	E	Y
F	S	T	E	G	T	R	U	A	R

24

Revision

Grammar

A Rewrite using capital letters and full stops. The first one is done for you.

I was awake very early that morning it was a tuesday in early december i was staying with my uncle tom at his villa in greece the first tremor came at about half past four it was a very mild one and it barely woke me up i was just nodding off again when the second one came my whole bed shook i could hear my cousin, carlos, starting to shout i jumped out of bed and ran to my balcony i saw doctor mouscouri falling about like a puppet suddenly my balcony started to shake violently the next thing i knew i was being flung forward i clung to a piece of the railing but i couldn't hold on the last thing i remember was my uncle tom as he tried to grab my arm i knew no more until i awoke in a hospital bed in athens

B Unscramble these sentences. Add capital letters.

1. went warsaw James' parents to.
2. bicycle won superb he racing the.
3. three fishing bought ago I a days new rod.
4. road on the slipped icy lady the old.
5. goal he football the winning the in scored game.
6. bookshop in Mary exciting novel bought the an.
7. girl won first prize the the small.
8. lap the overturned racing third on car the.
9. novel read the an man interesting.
10. cards we the morning hours until early the played.

C Rewrite using capital letters.

1. next monday is hallowe'en.
2. uncle sean gave me a present last tuesday.
3. i saw the president of france while in paris.
4. last june i visited my aunt halah.
5. he travelled to spain on new year's eve.
6. mr mandela was a famous president of south africa.
7. uncle richard's birthday is in may.
8. the sixth month of the year is june.
9. december is the last month of the year.

25

Writing

A Here are some earthquake words. Write eight more.

| gaping | quiver | Richter Scale | tremor | buried | falling | shake | scream |

_____   _____
_____   _____
_____   _____
_____   _____

B You are a reporter who has just arrived at the scene of an earthquake. You meet a girl with a bandage around her head. Write four questions that you might ask her and her answers.

_____
_____
_____
_____

C An earthquake has struck. You manage to escape from a three storey building. Suddenly you remember your pet dog has been left behind. Do you go back to get her? Write down the thoughts that go through your head.

Using Words

Language

A Try this feathered friends crossword.
Copy it onto squared paper.

Across

3. S _ i _ e: rhymes with swipe.
7. 24 of this bird were baked in a pie.
8. C _ _ ncr _ _ _: sounds like a breakfast cereal.
13.
14.
16. parsrow (anagram)
17. _ _ _ eon: a farm animal.

Down

1. One for sorrow.
2.
3.
4. _ _ _ _ daw: a boy's name.
5. renw (anagram)
6. Th _ _ _ _ : be in a hurry!
8. As the _ _ _ flies.
9. A type of clock.
10.
11.
12. neroh (anagram)
15. Hedwig is one.

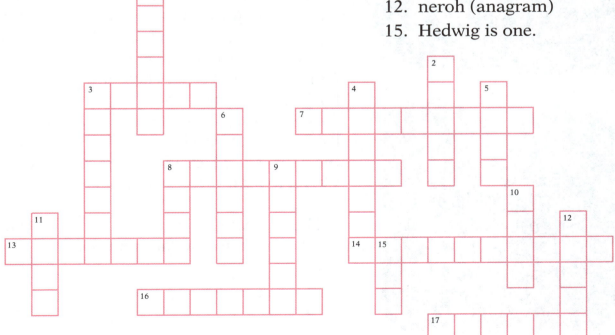

Reading

 A Read the text.

The Hummingbird

The tiny hummingbird gets its name from the sound it makes when flapping its wings. This colourful bird flaps its wings 50–60 times a second. How quickly can you click or snap your fingers in a second? Perhaps twice! By rapidly beating its wings, the hummingbird can remain in the same position, fly backwards and even rise straight up like a helicopter.

The hummingbird feeds on the nectar of flowers while **hovering** in flight. Its long thin beak and hairy tongue are specially suited to prod and probe the hearts of flowers. It also eats little insects.

This bird is remarkable for its **array** of red, blue and green colours. Although it is the smallest bird in the world, it will fearlessly attack crows and hawks that invade its territory and nest.

The cup-like nest it builds is an architectural wonder. A **mass** of grasses, mosses and **fibres** are woven together with strands of cobwebs, to form a tiny nest about the size of a walnut shell. The nest will hold two snow-white eggs. These are the smallest birds' eggs in the world.

When the eggs are hatched, the mother feeds the nestlings by thrusting her bill down their throats. Then, **vibrating** her body, she **regurgitates** the sweet nectar from her stomach.

The pretty hummingbird is found in North and South America and in Cuba.

28

Activities

A Answer these questions.

1. Where would you find the hummingbird?
2. How rapidly does it flap its wings?
3. How does it build its nest?
4. How does the mother feed her young?
5. What record does the hummingbird hold?
6. Why is the hummingbird remarkable?
7. What shape is its nest?
8. What does the hummingbird feed on?
9. How does the hummingbird get its name?
10. How many times can you click your fingers in ten seconds?

B Look up the words in *italics* in your dictionary. Write a sentence for each one.

C Summarise the story in your own words. Use about ten sentences.

D Write the correct verb.

1. The busy bee _____ (strolled, prowled, flitted) across the room.
2. The striped beetle _____ (charged, waded, crawled) under the stone.
3. The pretty butterfly _____ (hopped, hobbled, hovered) near the roses.
4. The croaking bullfrog _____ (leaped, limped, flew) into the deep pool.
5. The large spider _____ (strode, strolled, scurried) into its web.
6. The fat worm _____ (walked, waddled, wriggled) into its burrow.
7. The prickly hedgehog _____ (tickled, stung, prodded) the curious puppy.
8. The golden eagle _____ (grabbed, tore, trapped) its prey in its talons.
9. The timid snail _____ (flew, glided, scampered) along the damp grass.
10. The brown hen _____ (sniffed, pecked, gnawed) the pan of oats.

29

Phonics

Word Endings: 'ar' and 'er'

 A Write **er** or **ar** for each word.

st _ _   f _ _ m   lett _ _   slipp _ _   g _ _ den   sc _ _ f

butt _ _   c _ _ pet   lobst _ _   hamp _ _   sauc _ _   m _ _ ket

doll _ _   butch _ _   pill _ _   cell _ _   teach _ _   hang _ _

 B Write the correct word.

| jumper | beaver | player | golfer | cellar | bigger | hangar | beggar |

1. Aeroplanes are kept in a _____ .
2. The case of wine is in the _____ .
3. The _____ had been on the steps all day.
4. The dam was built by a _____ .
5. The _____ had a handicap of eighteen.
6. My ice cream cone was _____ than Tom's.
7. I tore a hole in my new _____ .
8. A point was scored by the new _____ on the team.

Adjectives

Grammar

> Adjectives are describing words.
> Example: The **hungry** fox went out on a **cold**, **dark** night.

  A **Underline all 14 adjectives.**

The new girl came into the big school. She had silky black hair and dark eyes. She held her shiny blue bag tightly. In the noisy playground were strange, staring faces. Then a little girl came up and took her to a quiet room where she met her smiling, welcoming teacher.

 B **Rewrite these sentences adding some adjectives. Use the help words in the box below.**

caring	old	buzzing	tired
timid	weary	low	dusty
juicy	comfortable	young	green
distant	wooden	high	smart
fragile	bloodthirsty	winding	new
shining	freshly-painted	silvery	fizzy
worried	red	dilapidated	sweet
thoughtful	vicious	lonely	speeding
humming	happy	neglected	crystal

1. The nurse smiled at the patient.
2. The dog barked at the moon.
3. The shark gnawed at the boat.
4. The car roared along the road.
5. The tourist stayed in the hotel.
6. The bus reversed into the van.
7. We ate strawberries and drank lemonade.
8. Two women carefully examined the glasses.
9. There were two chairs in the garden.
10. A swarm of bees settled on the branch.

Writing

A Write a short story about a storm at sea. Use the help words and ideas.

fierce storm	hovered	rescue operation
howling wind	sinking rapidly	coastguard
creaking	crew in peril (danger)	to safety
lone ship	hoisted (lifted)	wreckage
tossed about	ripped	helicopter
dangerous rocks	crashing waves	SOS signal

B Write a short story about witnessing an accident. Use the help words and ideas.

damp	screech of brakes	goods scattered
misty day	skidded	dashed
walking	spun across	rang for help
huge, powerful lorry	deafening (loud)	police
roared past	crash	hospital
sharp bend	overturned	ambulance

Language

Using Words

A Write two, too or to.

1. Jane found it _____ difficult _____ crawl between the _____ legs of the chair.
2. She went _____ the bathroom, turned on the _____ taps and flooded the place.
3. I was _____ frightened _____ tell mum the story.
4. When she broke the _____ cups, dad spoke gently _____ her, but her mother was not _____ pleased.
5. There was _____ much jam on the slice of bread.
6. The doll was _____ expensive _____ buy.
7. It was _____ early for the baby _____ go _____ bed.

B Write there or their.

1. The swallows were _____ with _____ friends the house martins.
2. Some birds obtain _____ food by digging with _____ bills.
3. The penguins fluttered _____ wings and waddled towards _____ pool.
4. The killer whales seized _____ victims in _____ jaws and disappeared.
5. _____ is a kingfisher on that rock over _____ .
6. _____ were hundreds of crows flying home to _____ nests in the wood.
7. The swallows built _____ nests _____ last year.

C Write where or were.

1. _____ did you go last night?
2. _____ there many elephants in the jungle?
3. They _____ at a football match two days ago.
4. We don't know _____ the teachers _____ .
5. We _____ standing _____ the river flowed into the sea.
6. The new houses are _____ the old markets _____ held.
7. _____ in Europe _____ you going to go on your holidays?

33

Reading

 A Read the story.

The Match Girl

It was Christmas Eve and snow lay deep on the ground. Night was falling and it was very, very cold. A little girl stood at the corner of a city street. Her clothes were in rags and her shoes were *tattered*. She held out small boxes of matches to the crowds of people passing by, but nobody bought any matches. She stood at the corner of the street all day, without a penny in her pocket.

The little girl grew colder and colder. In the evening she took *shelter* from the falling snow. She lit a match to keep herself warm.

The match burned brightly and, looking at it, the little girl saw a big room and a bright fire. When the flame went out, the big room *vanished*. Nothing was left but the cold and darkness.

The little girl lit another match. She saw the same room again. This time a crowd of happy children were sitting around a dinner table. On the table was a big, fat goose, but when the match went out, the room vanished. It was cold and dark once again.

The girl lit a third match. This time she saw a lovely Christmas tree with lights. When the match burned out, the lights rose into the sky and the match girl saw that they were stars.

One of the stars fell, and the child *recalled* that her dead grandmother had often told her that every time a star falls, a soul goes to Heaven.

As she lit another match, the girl saw her dear old grandmother. She kept on lighting match after match in case her grandmother would disappear like the dinner, the tree and the room.

"Do not go away, Granny," *pleaded* the match girl. "Stay with me or take me with you."

Her grandmother did not leave her. She reached down and took the little girl in her arms. They rose high into the sky and disappeared through the golden gates of Heaven.

In the morning, an old man found her little body in the doorway of a house, with all the burned matches beside her.

The people wondered why she had a beautiful smile on her face. They did not know of the lovely things she had seen or of the great joy that filled her heart when her grandmother came to take her home.

34

Activities

A Answer these questions.

1. What was the name of the story?
2. Which season was it?
3. Who was standing at the street corner?
4. How was she dressed?
5. What was she selling?
6. How many boxes of matches did she sell?
7. Why did she light a match?
8. What did she see when she lit the second match?
9. What fell from the sky?
10. Who came to visit the little match girl?
11. Where did her grandmother take her?
12. Who found the body of the little girl?
13. Why do you think the little girl had a smile on her face?
14. Make up a new title for the story.

B Look up the words in *italics* in your dictionary. Write a sentence for each one.

C Summarise the story in your own words. Use about ten sentences.

D Join each word with another word to make a compound word from the story.

1. no —— other   _____
2. match   gain   _____
3. grand → thing   _____
4. a   body   _____
5. no   way   _____
6. an   mother _____
7. a   self   _____
8. her   boxes   _____

35

Phonics

A Write the words. They all begin with the letter **n**.

1. The number of nines in 81. _____
2. The eleventh month of the year. _____
3. It is part of a pen. _____
4. This plant stings. _____
5. To move your head up and down. _____
6. Where a bird lays its eggs. _____
7. It is used to catch fish. _____
8. Opposite of wide. _____
9. Bees gather it from flowers. _____
10. A planet in our Solar System. _____
11. It is used for sewing. _____
12. Photographs are developed from these. _____
13. It is a famous river in Egypt. _____
14. A cat is said to have this number of lives. _____
15. Very dark blue. _____

B Unscramble the transport words. Find them in the wordsearch.

urtck _____
artin _____
plaeroane _____
ipsh _____
nocae _____
sub _____
biletomoau _____
torikemob _____
clecybi _____
teroosc _____

a	l	i	b	e	t	o	k	i	r
m	u	b	i	c	y	c	l	e	k
s	u	t	k	t	a	b	n	o	n
c	t	r	o	w	r	a	u	q	u
o	o	a	e	m	l	u	r	s	t
o	m	i	y	p	o	u	c	i	c
t	p	n	o	o	a	b	p	k	a
e	o	r	s	d	s	h	i	p	n
r	e	f	g	a	e	r	o	l	o
a	m	o	t	o	r	b	i	k	e

36

Grammar

Singular and Plural

> **Singular means only one. Plural means more than one.**
> **Examples:** One cat but two cats.
> One box but two boxes.

A Write the plural of the words in red.

1. She ate the biscuit on the tray.
2. The train sped through the valley.
3. She left the key in her pocket.
4. He bought the tie and the jumper.
5. The ray of light came through the window.
6. Snow covered the roof and chimney.
7. The boat sailed away from the quay.
8. The horse and jockey cleared the fence.

B Write these sentences in the singular.

1. The ladies read the books on the trains.
2. The dentists checked the children's teeth.
3. The babies wore nappies.
4. The foxes ate the salmon.
5. The fish were swimming in the deep pools.
6. The potatoes were served with fish.
7. The shops sell pliers and shears.
8. The farmers put the turkeys in the sheds.

C Write these sentences in the plural.

1. The boy put the cake in the oven.
2. The farmer lifted the rock from the field.
3. The cook prepared the dish in the oven.
4. The man put the box in the van.
5. His uncle gave him the watch.
6. The class found the shell on the beach.
7. The bird flew from the bush.
8. The plumber fixed the pipe in the cottage.

37

Writing

A **Make a list of six New Year's resolutions you might make.**

1. _____
2. _____
3. _____
4. _____
5. _____
6. _____

B **List the reasons why people sometimes abandon their pets.**

_____
_____
_____
_____
_____
_____

C **List the reasons why a pet might want to abandon their owner!**

_____
_____
_____
_____
_____
_____

Using Words

Language

A Rewrite these sentences using words from the box to replace **ate**.

| licked   nibbled   devoured   pecked   gobbled up   chewed |
| consumed   swallowed   munched   crunched |

1. The rabbit (ate) _____ the lettuce leaf.
2. The python (ate) _____ the wild dog.
3. The sheep (ate) _____ the green grass.
4. The mouse (ate) _____ the cheddar cheese.
5. The turkey (ate) _____ the mashed potatoes.
6. The hen (ate) _____ the seed.
7. The small girl (ate) _____ a lollipop.
8. The lion (ate) _____ the young deer.
9. The woman (ate) _____ the hard peanuts.
10. The child (ate) _____ the stick of liquorice.

B Rewrite these sentences using words from the box to replace **went**.

| marched   cantered   sneaked   wriggled   thundered   swung |
| waddled   trotted   scurried   slithered |

1. The train (went) _____ through the station.
2. The snake (went) _____ across the grass.
3. The fox (went) _____ into the chicken coop.
4. The worm (went) _____ along the ground.
5. The horse (went) _____ across the field.
6. The duck (went) _____ across the road.
7. The pony (went) _____ around the racetrack.
8. The monkey (went) _____ from branch to branch.
9. The rabbit (went) _____ into its burrow.
10. The soldier (went) _____ up the road.

Reading

 A Read the text.

Boeing 747

A Boeing 747 jumbo jet was once on its way from Indonesia to New Zealand with 247 passengers on board. The aircraft met with a thick, deadly cloud of dust and ash thrown into the sky by a *volcano*.

They were flying out over the sea at a height of 10,000 metres when the aircraft's four engines cut out, one by one.

A terrible silence fell over the aircraft. The quick-thinking pilot put his huge jet into a *glide* and turned back for the airport.

For a full thirteen minutes they glided through the air. Even without engines, this great aircraft seemed to take to the skies like a bird.

Suddenly the four engines started again. Thanks to this *magnificent* machine and its pilot, they were able to safely land half an hour later.

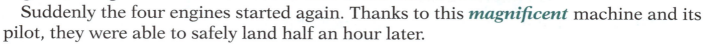

Here are some facts about jumbo jets:

1. The jumbo jet, or Boeing 747, is 70 metres long, six metres wide and 19.5 metres high.
2. It seats up to 500 passengers in one flight. In one year, a jumbo jet will take 150,000 people between France and America.
3. It can carry 214,000 litres of *fuel* which would be enough to keep a car running for a hundred years. In crossing from New York to London, a jumbo will use 90,000 litres of fuel.
4. It is made up of over four million parts and has over 160,000 kilometres of wires and *cables*.
5. Four massive jet engines are needed to get this 300 *tonne* machine into the air and 18 wheels are needed to support its weight on the ground.
6. A jumbo jet, flying to New York, will carry over 3000 kilograms of food and drinks to serve to passengers.
7. Flying at a height of 10,600 metres, the Boeing 747 cruises along at a speed of 912 kilometres per hour (560 mph).

Activities

A Answer these questions.

1. How heavy is the jumbo jet?
2. How much fuel does it carry?
3. How many passengers does it carry?
4. What height and speed does it reach?
5. What did a jumbo jet once meet on its way to New Zealand?
6. Why do you think its engines cut out?
7. What did the pilot do?

B Look up the words in *italics* in your dictionary. Write a sentence for each one.

C Summarise the story in your own words. Use about ten sentences.

D Find these 15 airport words in the wordsearch.

aeorplane
airport
arrivals
baggage
boarding card
check-in
departures
hangar
jumbo jet
luggage
passenger
passport
pilot
runway
take-off

j	a	a	p	m	h	a	n	g	a	r	d	u
l	f	l	d	e	p	a	r	t	u	r	e	s
s	k	u	g	e	q	e	n	t	a	t	y	n
l	l	g	r	o	g	i	v	c	e	a	t	t
z	q	g	u	a	–	q	g	j	r	r	a	w
d	f	a	g	k	p	n	o	e	o	r	k	h
e	x	g	c	x	i	b	g	p	p	i	e	i
b	a	e	n	d	m	n	s	i	l	v	–	x
b	h	i	r	u	e	s	j	l	a	a	o	g
c	p	a	j	s	a	q	r	o	n	l	f	h
i	o	u	s	p	x	y	e	t	e	s	f	s
b	t	a	i	r	p	o	r	t	b	y	p	b
p	p	r	u	n	w	a	y	u	t	q	v	u

41

Phonics

Word Endings: 'or', 'ur' and 'ir'

A Unjumble the letters and write the **or** words.

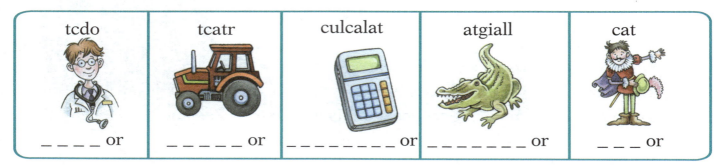

tcdo	tcatr	culcalat	atgiall	cat
_ _ _ _ or	_ _ _ _ _ or	_ _ _ _ _ _ _ or	_ _ _ _ _ _ _ or	_ _ _ or

B Write the missing letters.

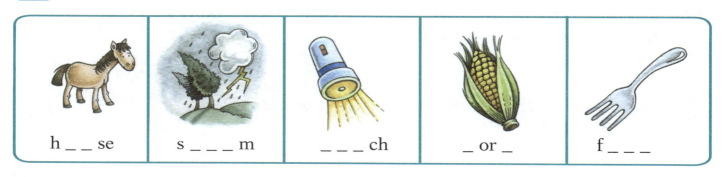

| h _ _ se | s _ _ _ m | _ _ _ ch | _ or _ | f _ _ _ |

C Use **ir** or **ur** to make a word.

1. c   l   _____
2. b   d   _____
3. h   t   _____
4. b   n   _____
5. t   f   _____

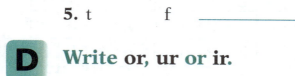

D Write **or**, **ur** or **ir**.

1. first
2. b _ _ d
3. g _ _ l
4. b _ _ th
5. Sat _ _ day
6. Th _ _ sday
7. visit _ _
8. f _ _ get
9. mot _ _
10. w _ _ k
11. sh _ _ t
12. th _ _ d
13. bl _ _
14. c _ _ ry

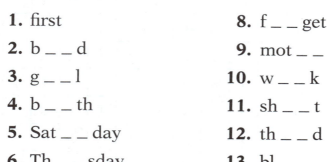

Grammar

Masculine and Feminine

> A word is masculine if it refers to a male person – **king**.
> A word is feminine if it refers to a female person – **queen**.

 A Write the masculine form of the coloured words.

1. The queen spoke to her daughter.
2. The aunt spoke to her niece.
3. The bride listened to her mother.
4. The wife praised the woman.
5. Her granddaughter became a princess.
6. The widow met her sister at the airport.
7. The girl had no grandmother.
8. The stepmother spoke to her daughter-in-law.

> A word is masculine if it refers to a male animal – **stallion**.
> A word is feminine if it refers to a female animal – **mare**.

B Write the feminine form of the coloured words.

1. The drake swam in the pond.
2. The ram was grazing in the field.
3. The lion was dozing in the shade.
4. The peacock strutted on the lawn.
5. The billy goat ate my hat.
6. The fox attacked the chickens.
7. The gander made lots of noise.
8. The colt stayed close to the fence.

C Write these words under the correct heading.

ram   fox
girl   boy
prince   duck
princess uncle
nephew   colt
vixen   niece
aunt   filly

Masculine	Feminine

43

Writing

Proofreading

A Proofread this paragraph. Rewrite it correctly.

wunce apon a time, their were sheeps in a big feild their wear so many sheeps that teh framer kept loosing count he tryed putting then all intoo won field and counting them as thay jumbed over the fence but he only got two twenty-too and then he felt a sleep

B Proofread this paragraph. Rewrite it correctly.

the most commin tipes of owls in irland are the barn-owl and the long-eard owl. the short-eard owl is a Winter visiter butt also has being knowen too nest here. owls are nocturnel. there large eye's can sea verey well in the dark. There eyes is at the frunt off the head, not at the sid.

C Proofread this paragraph. Rewrite it correctly. You may need to use more than one paragraph.

Sometimes latter, the kings musitiun brok his harp He searched evrywere for the wood of a willo tree to make a new harp at last he found a willo treee by a streem He cut down the tree and made a beutiful harp from the soft would
That knight there was a big feest in Knig larrys palace All the nobles and lords wre in the great hall The king ordered his harper to play sum musik for his guests But when the harper plucked the strings, the harp began to sing loudly: "king larry has the hears of a horse the ears of a horse"
There was sylence int he great hal

D Write ten sentences with a deliberate mistake in each sentence. Ask your partner to find the mistakes.

44

Using Words

Language

A Write the correct group term. Use the words in the box.

| shoal | litter | flight | skulk | school | herd | brood | flock | team |
| pride | nest | pack | troop | hive | swarm | gaggle | | |

1. a _____ of monkeys
2. a _____ of insects
3. a _____ of chickens
4. a _____ of birds
5. a _____ of foxes
6. a _____ of zebra
7. a _____ of mice
8. a _____ of geese
9. a _____ of fish
10. a _____ of lions
11. a _____ of pups
12. a _____ of wolves
13. a _____ of whales
14. a _____ of bees
15. a _____ of swallows
16. a _____ of horses

B Finish these sentences.

1. The fleet of ships _____.
2. The flock of sheep _____.
3. A herd of buffaloes _____.
4. The company of dancers _____.
5. An army of soldiers _____.
6. The class of children _____.
7. A choir of singers _____.
8. The bunch of grapes _____.

C Write a group name for each set.

1. fir, oak, ash, chestnut _____
2. shark, salmon, trout, plaice _____
3. Alps, Rockies, Himalayas, Andes _____
4. Atlantic, Pacific, Indian, Arctic _____
5. Japan, Ireland, Greenland, France _____
6. New York, Moscow, Beijing, London _____
7. canoe, punt, barge, catamaran _____
8. guitar, flute, violin, mandolin _____
9. viper, python, cobra, asp _____
10. Pluto, Venus, Mars, Saturn _____

Reading

 A Read the story.

One Man's Horse

One day a king, known as the Caliph, *disguised* himself as an ordinary person and set off on horseback to find out how well his kingdom was being run. On the way, he came across an old, lame beggar by the side of the road.

"Good traveller," said the beggar, "I'm on my way to Bassora. Let me ride with you."

So the Caliph helped the beggar up onto the horse's back. When they reached Bassora, the Caliph asked the beggar to get off the horse, but the beggar refused.

"Get off yourself," he said. "In Bassora we are both strangers. No-one knows whose horse this is, and it will be your word against mine."

The Caliph *wondered* what he should do. "If I throw the beggar off the horse," he thought, "he will make a big fuss. A crowd will gather and people will tell me to give the old man his horse back. If I give the beggar money, I might get my horse back, but the old man might *cheat* someone else in the same way. If I ask a cadi (judge) to decide the matter, I may lose my horse, but at least I'll find out how well the cadi of Bassora does his job."

And so the Caliph and the beggar went to see the cadi of Bassora.

"Your Honour," said the Caliph, "I am a *traveller* from a faraway country. A few miles outside your city, I met this lame beggar. I took pity on him and brought him into the city on my horse. He now claims that my horse belongs to him."

The cadi turned to the beggar. "What have you got to say?" he said.

"The horse is mine," answered the beggar. "I am just a poor, lame old man. If you take my horse away from me, I don't know what I shall do." The beggar *pretended* to cry.

"Leave the horse with one of my soldiers, and return to this courtroom tomorrow morning."

The next morning, the cadi said to the beggar, "Why have you repaid this man's *kindness* with *ingratitude*?" He then turned to the Caliph. "Good traveller, the horse is yours. Take it, and continue your journey."

"Your judgment is excellent!" said the Caliph. "But how could you tell who owned the horse?"

"Last night I put your horse in a stable that you and the beggar would have to pass on your way to court today. This morning I went to the stable. When the beggar passed, the horse didn't look up. But when you passed the open door, he stretched out his head and neighed as horses only do when their master approaches. So you see, the matter was very simple after all."

"Simple?" cried the Caliph. "You are the wisest man I have ever met! I am the Caliph. I need a man like you in my capital city. I shall make you the Grand Cadi!"

46

Activities

A **Answer these questions.**

1. Why did the Caliph want to travel around his kingdom?
2. Why do you think he chose to go in disguise?
3. What act of kindness did the Caliph carry out on his journey?
4. Why did the Caliph decide not to throw the beggar off the horse?
5. Why did the Caliph decide not to give the beggar money?
6. Why did the Caliph want the cadi to decide who should keep the horse?
7. How did the cadi find out that the horse belonged to the Caliph?
8. Why do you think the Caliph make the cadi of Bassora the Grand Cadi?

B **Look up the words in *italics* in your dictionary. Write a sentence for each one.**

C **Summarise the story in your own words. Use about ten sentences.**

D **Can you find ten occupations in the wordsearch?**

m	u	s	i	c	i	a	n	d	a	n	b	s
t	o	l	i	p	c	d	e	e	p	u	f	h
n	o	g	h	i	j	p	h	n	o	r	k	o
a	b	d	o	c	t	o	r	t	r	s	s	p
m	b	v	m	n	o	s	e	i	t	e	s	k
e	l	e	q	r	h	t	m	s	m	s	e	e
r	e	t	u	c	v	m	r	t	g	x	r	e
i	r	a	a	y	z	a	a	a	n	b	t	p
f	e	e	c	d	e	n	f	f	g	h	c	e
2	t	i	j	f	r	e	k	a	b	k	a	r

47

Phonics

G or J?

A Write the missing letters.

_ ar   _ enie   _ et   _ ig _ _ _   _ ener _ _

_ ira _ _ _   _ elly _ _ _ _   _ erb _ _   _ ym   _ u _

B Write g or j.

1. Rajan's father is a ma_ician.
2. The _ockey wore very bright colours.
3. Kate loves telling _okes.
4. The _eneral is a senior officer in the army.
5. The _iant could not find a pair of _eans to fit him.
6. The children en_oyed being on sta_e.
7. The tiger prowled through the _ungle.
8. Leanne likes _am on her bread.

C Write the correct word.

1. This g word can make people sick. (4) _____
2. This j word means a funny little story. (4) _____
3. This g word is an animal with a long neck. (7) _____
4. This j word is something sweet to spread on bread. (3) _____
5. This j word is a wobbly dessert. (5) _____
6. This g word is a precious stone. (3) _____
7. This g word is a school subject. (9) _____
8. This j word is a person who works in a law court. (5) _____

Nouns

Grammar

> The word **noun** means name. A noun is the name of any:
> 1. person – **John**.
> 2. place – **desert**.
> 3. thing – **frog**.

A Write three nouns for each group.

1. Clothes
2. Sports
3. Countries
4. Animals
5. Furniture
6. Rivers
7. Mountains
8. Pets

B Write the correct noun for each of the following.

1. A person who gives lessons.
2. The traditional building of the Inuit.
3. An animal with no legs and a forked tongue.
4. A person who fights fires.
5. The place where a clown perfoms.
6. The animal known as the King of the Jungle.
7. A thing that is used for measuring time.
8. A person who travels in space.

C Circle the noun that is the odd one out. Give a reason.

1. trout, robin, herring, cod, pike
2. rabbit, badger, otter, fox, hare
3. peach, pineapple, pear, potato, plum
4. oyster, mussel, octopus, periwinkle, whelk
5. kangaroo, mule, pony, donkey
6. necklace, ring, bracelet, lipstick

Writing

A You found this map in the attic. Write about the adventure when you and your best friend decided to go in search of the treasure.

50

Using Words

Language

A Write the opposites. Use the help words.

> entrance   found   hate   sell   down   go   pull   many   dead   under
> safe   awake   poverty   rude   sweet   everywhere

1. few _____
2. exit _____
3. buy _____
4. nowhere _____
5. dangerous _____
6. bitter _____
7. lost _____
8. up _____
9. over _____
10. wealth _____
11. asleep _____
12. push _____
13. love _____
14. stop _____
15. alive _____
16. polite _____

B Choose a suitable **colour** word for each sentence.

> black   brown   evergreen   grey   golden   hazel   red   white   blue
> tawny   purple   pink   silver-grey   green-eyed   blue   speckled

1. The gardener sprayed the _____ roses.
2. The _____ leaves withered and died.
3. The _____ trout leaped out of the water.
4. The elephant has _____ ivory tusks.
5. The _____ daffodils swayed in the evening breeze.
6. The _____ beetle laid her eggs under a mossy stone.
7. The hills were covered with _____ heather.
8. The _____ firs were covered with snow.
9. The _____ owl hooted in the woods.
10. The small squirrel cracked the _____ nuts.
11. A _____ mist hung over the valley.
12. The lark sang in the clear _____ sky.
13. The _____ stallion roamed the prairies.
14. The _____ monster rose out of the sea.
15. The hedge sparrow's nest had four _____ eggs in it.
16. The salmon's flesh is a pale _____ colour.

Reading

 Read the text.

The Polar Bear

The polar bear lives in the frozen lands of the Arctic. The Inuit call him 'Nanook'. The bear's short legs, long body and slender snout give the *impression* of a slow-moving animal. Do not be *deceived*! Though weighing over 700 kilograms, the polar bear can travel at speeds of more than 48 kilometres per hour!

He is so strong that a single blow of his mighty paw can break the neck of an ox.

Polar bears are expert divers and swimmers. You may meet them 160–300 kilometres out in the ocean calmly riding along on a floating iceberg or swimming gracefully in the freezing water. Thick layers of fat allow them to remain a long time in such cold water.

Polar bears have special eyelids that shield their eyes from the glare of snow and ice. The soles of their feet are padded with fur to prevent them from slipping on the ice and packed snow.

The polar bear's favourite meal is seal flesh. This huge white hunter of the Arctic follows the migrating seals. He is able to pick up the scent of seal blubber as far away as 30 kilometres. When a polar bear finds a seal's breathing hole in the ice, he sits patiently near the mouth of the hole with his paw raised, ready to strike. The moment the seal appears, the bear's mighty claws of steel come down. He seldom misses his target.

The deadly killer whale is the polar bear's greatest enemy. In the water, the bear is no match for this huge sea mammal. They must also keep a sharp look-out for their enemy, the walrus, who is bigger and stronger than they are. Sometimes the fearless polar bear will sneak up on a sleeping walrus and hit it with a block of frozen ice.

The female bear gives birth to one or two cubs in a deep cave or snow tunnel. The newborn cubs weigh less than a kilogram and are blind and naked. The *devoted* mother protects her young and feeds them throughout the long winter. They remain with her for about two years. During this time, the female bear is very dangerous and will bravely defend her young against attack. When the young polar bears are strong enough, they wander off to lead their own *solitary* lives in the land of snow and ice.

Activities

A Answer these questions.

1. In what part of the world does the polar bear live?
2. Why is he called the 'white hunter'?
3. How is it shown that the polar bear has great strength?
4. Why does he not freeze in the Arctic waters?
5. What protection does he have from the glare of the snow?
6. Why does the polar bear not slip on the ice?
7. What is the bear's favourite food?
8. What enemies does the polar bear have?
9. Where are the cubs born?

B Look up the words in *italics* in your dictionary. Write a sentence for each one.

C Summarise the story in your own words. Use about ten sentences.

D Find these 12 Arctic words in the wordsearch.

Inuit
Nanook
blubber
claw
cub
fish
iceberg
mammal
polar bear
seals
snow
walrus

q	N	i	w	d	a	z	l	g	h	i	g
r	a	w	m	m	y	v	r	s	r	n	r
p	n	i	a	z	d	o	i	w	g	n	c
t	o	g	m	x	e	f	v	g	q	h	m
g	o	l	m	d	p	s	w	g	k	x	h
w	k	r	a	c	l	o	r	o	u	z	v
v	h	s	l	r	n	e	b	y	l	v	m
u	j	I	n	s	b	l	u	b	b	e	r
f	c	n	v	e	q	e	s	w	f	k	k
z	e	u	c	a	p	w	a	l	r	u	s
d	a	i	b	l	e	l	q	r	i	q	r
t	h	t	n	s	c	w	n	y	k	s	f

53

Phonics

Silent Letters: 'g' and 't'

A Try this **silent g** wordsearch.

gnome
gnaw
gnarled
gnu
gnashing
sign
reign
resign
design

v	s	i	g	n	h	w	f	d
d	b	g	n	a	w	l	t	e
e	h	l	o	b	u	m	n	s
l	t	b	m	n	n	c	p	i
r	q	r	e	i	g	n	t	g
a	r	e	s	i	g	n	a	n
n	j	p	x	v	l	f	n	q
g	n	a	s	h	i	n	g	w

B Write the correct **silent t** word.

castle   wrestle   thistle   nestle   fasten   gristle   whistle   listen
rustle   bristles

1. The queen lives in a _____ .
2. The _____ has prickly leaves and a purple flower.
3. The kitten tried to _____ in the basket.
4. The referee blew the _____ at half time.
5. The teacher told us to _____ carefully.
6. The leaves began to _____ in the trees.
7. The _____ on the brush were falling out.
8. You should always _____ your seat belt.
9. The man tried to _____ the thief to the ground.
10. _____ is the tough tissue in meat.

Grammar

Nouns

> Remember: A noun is the name of a person, place, animal or thing.

A **Write suitable nouns.**

1. The cat has four _____ and two _____ .
2. Mice eat _____ and _____ .
3. A young dog is called a _____ .
4. The swan swam gracefully in the _____ .
5. The goat butted the _____ with its horns.
6. The ant carried _____ to the _____ .
7. The _____ is the tallest animal in the world.
8. The hunter shot a wild _____ in the _____ .
9. The wolf and the _____ live in the _____ .
10. An elephant's long nose is called a _____ .

B **Underline the nouns.**

1. Rabbits dig burrows in the ground.
2. My dog lives in a kennel.
3. The bullfrog leaped into the pond.
4. There are many giraffes and lions in Africa.
5. The eagle has a nest in the mountains.
6. Honeybees make honey in hives.
7. John Smith bought a donkey and a goat.
8. The sheepdog buried a bone in the garden.
9. The spider spun a web in the garage.
10. The wasp stung Mina on the nose.

C **Unscramble the nouns.**

1. kdonye _____
2. yks _____
3. epcoumtr _____
4. galf _____
5. cihdl _____
6. leas _____
7. fclif _____
8. pihs _____
9. elbep _____
10. ddelas _____
11. llesh _____
12. abehc _____
13. slmiey _____
14. koob _____
15. tawre _____
16. eltetr _____
17. aesllug _____
18. csohlo _____

Writing

A Why are these things dangerous to do?

1. Ride your bike at night without lights.
2. Walk along an unlit road in dark clothes at night.
3. Drive over the 30 mph speed limit.
4. Use a mobile phone when driving.
5. Overtake on a bend.
6. Travel in a car without wearing a seatbelt.
7. Play football in the road.

B Think of a poster campaign or television campaign encouraging safety on the roads. Write about ten sentences.

Using Words

Language

A Write the correct word.

snail ox gold pancake hatter owl fiddle hills ice bee

1. As mad as a _____
2. As slow as a _____
3. As cold as _____
4. As fit as a _____
5. As good as _____
6. As flat as a _____
7. As strong as an _____
8. As wise as an _____
9. As old as the _____
10. As busy as a _____

B Write the correct word.

daisy monkey road coal won oak snow beam bought competition judge ant owl swan ballerina hare morning happy week flat

1. I woke up this _____ as fresh as a _____ .
2. The table he _____ was as sturdy as an _____ .
3. He _____ the race because he ran as fast as a _____ .
4. Her hair was as black as _____ and her skin was as white as _____ .
5. The gymnast on the _____ was as agile as a _____ .
6. I will be as busy as an _____ for the rest of the _____ .
7. After winning the _____ she was as _____ as a lark.
8. The High Court _____ was as wise as an _____ .
9. The cyclist was glad the long _____ was as _____ as a pancake.
10. The _____ dancing on stage was as graceful as a _____ .

C Choose the correct word.

1. As blind as a _____ (rat, bat, cat).
2. As graceful as a _____ (donkey, swan, elephant).
3. As slow as a _____ (hare, fox, snail).
4. As gentle as a _____ (lamb, hawk, tiger).
5. As strong as an _____ (mule, ox, dog).
6. As sly as a _____ (robin, hawk, fox).
7. As hungry as a _____ (mouse, fox, wolf).
8. As brave as a _____ (monkey, deer, lion).

Reading

 A Read the text.

Walk on the Moon

On 20 July 1969, people all over the world sat and watched their television sets. Two men from Earth had landed on the Moon and were about to *disembark* their spacecraft and step onto the Moon's *surface*.

The astronauts were well-equipped. Their specially designed spacesuits would save them from the great heat outside their spaceship. They had air tanks on their backs that would help them breathe when they walked on the Moon.

When they were ready, they slowly opened the door of their small spaceship. More than six hours after landing on the Moon, a grainy black and white picture was *transmitted* live from the Moon. It showed a white shape slowly moving among the shadows as Neil Armstrong exited the *lunar* module and started to climb down the short ladder. As he put his foot down on the Moon he said, "That's one small step for man – one giant leap for *mankind*." Neil Armstrong had become the first person to set foot on the Moon.

Astronaut Edwin E 'Buzz' Aldrin, followed Armstrong down the ladder. The Moon was covered in dust, which stuck to their boots and there were small rocks *strewn* about.

At first, it was not easy to walk on the Moon. The astronauts had to get used to the weightlessness of being on the Moon. If you weigh sixty kilograms on Earth, you will weigh only ten kilograms on the Moon. Soon, however, they got used to being so light and began to hop, skip and jump about. But they only had enough air to give them three hours on the Moon. There were rocks to collect and tests to be done. When they were finished, they left a message on the dusty ground. It said, 'Here, men from planet Earth set foot upon the Moon, July 1969. We came in peace for all mankind.'

Activities

A **Answer these questions.**

1. Why were people watching TV on 20 July 1969?
2. Why did the men wear spacesuits?
3. What did they carry on their backs?
4. Who stepped onto the Moon first and what did he say?
5. Why was it not easy to walk on the Moon?
6. Why did they not stay longer?
7. What was the message they left there?
8. Why do you think the spacemen wanted to bring rocks back to Earth?

B **Look up the words in *italics* in your dictionary. Write a sentence for each one.**

C **Describe the Moon in your own words. Use about ten sentences.**

D **Choose the correct word.**

| craters   millions   orbit   boiling   thousand   sound |
| freeze   surface |

1. Some people believe that the Moon was once part of the Earth and broke away _____ of years ago.
2. The Moon's _____ has high mountains, deep valleys and wide flat spaces.
3. Huge holes called _____ can be many kilometres wide with walls two kilometres high.
4. Because there is no air on the Moon, there is no _____ .
5. One day on the Moon lasts for two weeks. The rocks become hotter than _____ water.
6. One night on the Moon also lasts two weeks. It becomes so cold that a person would _____ to death within minutes.
7. The Moon is about 383 _____ kilometres away from Earth.
8. It takes the Moon 27 days, 7 hours, 43 minutes and 12 seconds to _____ the Earth.

Phonics

Silent Letters: 'b' and 'l'

A Write the missing letters.

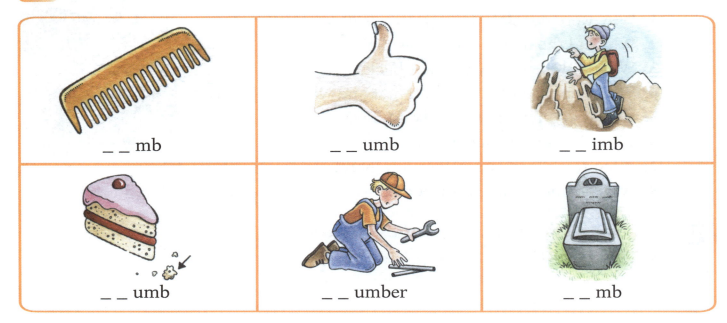

_ _ mb   _ _ umb   _ _ imb

_ _ umb   _ _ umber   _ _ mb

B Choose the correct word.

1. The kitchen flooded so I called a _____ (plumber, climber).
2. My mum told me to _____ (limb, comb, tomb) my hair.
3. Birds ate the _____ (comb, crumbs) on the table.
4. My baby sister sucks her _____ (tomb, thumb).
5. I'm going to _____ (crumb, climb) to the top of the hill.
6. Mary had a little _____ (limb, lamb, climb).
7. There are lots of old _____ (combs, tombs) in our local graveyard.
8. The dentist _____ (numbed, combed) my gums.

C Join the silent l words to their meaning.

1. calf   quiet
2. half   used for writing on a chalkboard
3. walk   one of two equal parts
4. palm   inside part of the hand
5. calm   to speak to someone
6. yolk   to move along on foot
7. talk   the yellow part of an egg
8. chalk   a young elephant

Grammar

Adjectives

> A sentence can often be made more interesting by adding one or more **adjectives**.
> Example: The girl drank the water.
> The **thirsty** girl drank the **cool** water.

A Choose the correct adjective.

> touching   generous   small   kind   big   soft   old   cold
> feathery   shivering   outstretched

He was an _____ man and he lived in the _____ house next to ours. He was very _____ to the birds during the _____ months of winter. Each morning he used to take them _____ morsels of _____ bread. The _____ birds used to perch on his _____ arm and eat the crumbs of bread. It was a very _____ sight to see this _____ man with his _____ friends around him.

B Find the adjectives.

The Murray family rose early on the first morning of their holiday in Scotland. The weather was warm and sunny – a perfect day for a nice picnic at the seaside. The happy and excited children helped their parents prepare a big feast of tasty sandwiches and home-made cakes. After a quick breakfast, they set off on foot for a small, sandy beach about a mile from their thatched cottage. Already, the clear, blue sky was filled with the sweet, joyful song of tiny larks. As they strolled down the dusty road, their eager eyes gazed upon the broad, calm ocean.

C Find the adjectives.

1. Their tired eyes looked out across the vast desert.
2. Our simple but clever plan was to hide in the wooden barn.
3. The young boy rode down the dusty road on his red bicycle.
4. They tied a long string to a red rosy apple.
5. For my birthday I had a delicious cake and a brilliant party.
6. The hungry thrush fed on a fat, juicy worm.
7. The little girl's pet rabbit loved its cosy new home.
8. The first train was fast and comfortable.
9. The thin ice cracked under the weight of the heavy skater.
10. The silver salmon slept in the deep, dark pool.

Using Words

Language

A **Write of or off.**

1. The referee ordered the player _____ the field at the end _____ the game.
2. The tall runner set _____ before the rest _____ the other runners.
3. The fox ran _____ with two _____ mother's hens.
4. The man took _____ his coat and jumped _____ the rock.
5. Aba, the baby _____ the family, was afraid _____ the big dog next door.
6. Lin turned _____ the television before going _____ to bed.
7. The two _____ them strolled _____ down the dusty road.
8. At the far end _____ the field the player was carried _____ on a stretcher.
9. The Ace _____ Spades was the card that fell _____ the table.
10. The Fourth _____ July celebrations went _____ without a hitch.

B **Write are or our.**

1. Where _____ _____ schoolbags?
2. They _____ coming to _____ house this weekend.
3. They _____ enjoying the party.
4. The windows _____ open because it's a hot day.
5. When _____ you coming to stay at _____ house?
6. There _____ three bedrooms in _____ bungalow.
7. There _____ seven days in a week.
8. _____ school has ten classrooms.
9. _____ Egyptian relatives are planning to visit _____ country.
10. When _____ _____ holidays beginning?
11. When _____ friends arrive we _____ going to have a barbecue.
12. _____ the results of _____ tests ready yet?

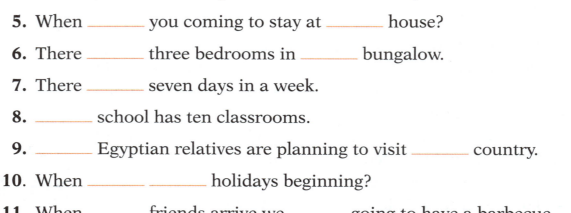

62

Using Words

Language

A **Write a or an.**

1. We saw _____ unusual crocodile near _____ marshy swamp.
2. I watched _____ enormous reptile kill _____ elephant in _____ cave.
3. She saw _____ swarm of giant ants attacking _____ nest of cockroaches.
4. _____ huge frog, with _____ long tail, leaped into _____ deep hole.
5. _____ eight-tonne dinosaur had _____ small brain.
6. _____ Iguanodon laid _____ egg the size of _____ football.
7. _____ giant toad swallowed _____ large fly.
8. _____ Allosaurus was _____ giant dinosaur.
9. _____ Archaeopteryx was _____ flying bird.
10. I sent _____ old dagger to _____ friend in the museum.

> **It's/its**
> it's **means** it is – It's **a lovely day.**
> its **means belonging to** – The doll is wearing its **hat.**

B **Write it's or its.**

1. The budgie is singing in _____ cage.
2. The windows are open because _____ a hot day.
3. "_____ not fair," moaned Paul.
4. The dog is burying _____ bone.
5. _____ dangerous to cross the road when _____ busy.
6. _____ an awful pity that _____ raining!
7. _____ my birthday on Friday.
8. The dog injured _____ leg and now _____ at the vet's.
9. _____ no use, _____ plug is broken so we cannot turn it on.
10. A cat licks _____ fur when _____ cleaning itself.

63

Reading

 Read the story.

Planet Problem!

"Mercury, Venus, em, Earth, em, Mars, em, em ... oh, it's *futile*! I'll never be able to remember all nine!" sighed Alice as she flopped her head down onto her hands.

Alice had spent all afternoon learning about the *Galaxy*, the Milky Way and Mars. She had also spent all afternoon thinking about chocolate, which didn't help.

The doorbell rang and Alice got up to answer it. It was Cian from next door. "Great," thought Alice as she opened the door, "Cian can help me learn the planets." Cian sat at the big table in the kitchen, which was *draped* with Alice's schoolbooks.

"I'm trying really hard to learn the planets for my science test tomorrow," Alice complained, "but sometimes I find it difficult to remember things."

"What you need is mnemonics," said Cian, helpfully.

"Nem what?" asked Alice.

"Mnemonics," repeated Cian. "It is a way of helping you remember something. It is also the only word in the English language that begins with the letters 'mn', the 'm' being silent."

"Mr Know-it-all!" laughed Alice. "Tell me how it works!"

Cian explained how using rhymes and songs or making words from other words or sentences can help you remember.

Alice was still confused so Cian gave her some examples. He explained how singing the alphabet to the tune of 'Twinkle, Twinkle, Little Star' made it easier for children to learn the alphabet. He also told her how the sentence 'Richard of York gave battle in *vain*' made it easier to learn the order of the colours of the rainbow.

"That's great," said Alice, "but how can I remember the planets?"

"My very easy *method* just sums up nine planets," smiled Cian.

"That's great, Cian," said Alice, getting *frustrated*, "but what is it?"

"That's it! **M**y, **V**ery, **E**asy, **M**ethod, **J**ust, **S**ums, **U**p, **N**ine, **P**lanets. Mercury, Venus, Earth, Mars, Jupiter, Saturn, Uranus, Neptune, Pluto!" smiled Cian.

"That's brilliant!" shouted Alice. "I'll never forget my planets again!"

64

Activities

A Answer these questions.

1. What was the name of the story?
2. What had Alice been trying to learn all afternoon?
3. What else had Alice been thinking about and why?
4. Who was at the door?
5. According to Cian, what did Alice need?
6. Name one example of mnemonics given by Cian.
7. What is the sentence Cian uses to remember the planets?
8. Name three other things people do to help them remember something.

B Look up the words in *italics* in your dictionary. Write a sentence for each one.

C Summarise the story in your own words. Use about ten sentences.

D Choose the correct colour or planet.

| red orange yellow green blue indigo violet |
| Mercury Venus Earth Mars Jupiter Saturn Uranus Neptune Pluto |

1. The gardener sprayed the _____ roses.
2. _____ is a planet and the name of a chocolate bar.
3. The _____ daffodils swayed in the evening breeze.
4. _____ shares its name with the Roman god of water and the sea.
5. Sunrua is an anagram of _____ .
6. The stones were covered with _____ moss.
7. _____ is encircled by a series of rings.
8. _____ is a deep blue colour.
9. _____ is the largest planet in the Solar System.
10. My _____ jeans ran in the wash and made everything purple.
11. In the Solar System, _____ is the furthest from the Sun.
12. _____ shares its name with the Roman goddess of love.
13. My favourite drink is freshly-squeezed _____ juice.
14. _____ is found inside thermometers.
15. The huge monster rose out of the deep, _____ sea.
16. I live on _____ .

65

Fun Time

Language

 A Write the words. They all begin with the letter F.

1. Four nines plus two sevens. _____
2. If it's not true, it's _____.
3. Another name for a violin. _____
4. Another name for leaves. _____
5. Half of thirty. _____
6. A country in the European Union. _____
7. This is the name given to a young horse. _____
8. They grow on birds. _____
9. The shortest month of the year. _____
10. The entrance hall of a cinema, hotel or theatre. _____
11. To move or act restlessly. _____
12. Water does this at zero degrees Celsius. _____
13. She is a young, female horse. _____

 B Unscramble the names of the planets. Find them in the wordsearch.

thEar _____
unStar _____
itperJu _____
rsaM _____
eVsun _____
tluPo _____
cuMerry _____
peteNun _____
sanrUu _____

S	E	r	t	s	N	e	p	t	u
n	a	P	l	M	e	r	m	y	U
M	r	t	J	u	p	i	t	e	r
a	t	a	u	o	t	M	r	E	a
r	h	s	t	r	u	c	a	a	n
d	l	u	M	s	n	u	E	r	u
o	l	V	u	y	e	r	P	t	s
P	n	n	S	a	t	y	l	l	o
h	e	M	e	r	c	u	r	y	u
V	J	u	p	V	e	n	u	l	c

66

Grammar

Homonyms

> **Homonyms** are words that are pronounced alike but are different in spelling and meaning.
> Example: tail and tale.

A Choose the correct word.

1. It was _____ o'clock before I _____ a morsel of food. (ate, eight)
2. He hid the _____ amount of his savings in a deep _____. (hole, whole)
3. When you _____ that red _____ it will grow into a tree. (berry, bury)
4. It was an _____ later that _____ boat departed from the quay. (our, hour)
5. Everyone _____ that he bought a _____ bicycle. (new, knew)
6. She _____ the title on the cover of the _____ book. (red, read)
7. The trainer _____ that the player's _____ is fractured. (nose, knows)
8. The ram and the _____ stood near the _____ tree. (yew, ewe)
9. Harry _____ like to go for a nature walk through the _____. (would, wood)
10. She _____ the ball _____ the window. (threw, through)

B Choose the correct word.

1. Grate, great   Which belongs to a fireplace?   _____
2. Teem, team   Which is a group of people?   _____
3. Pair, pear, pare   Which is a fruit?   _____
4. Leek, leak   Which is a vegetable?   _____
5. Bow, bough   Which is a branch?   _____

C Write the homonyms.

Seven days	_____	Feeble	_____
Sixty minutes	_____	Belonging to us	_____
Expensive	_____	An animal	_____
Shines in sky	_____	A male child	_____
Pull (e.g. car)	_____	Of the foot	_____
Tied to a mast	_____	Selling of goods	_____
A story	_____	Part of a dog	_____
Useless	_____	Blood vessel	_____
Seaside	_____	Type of a tree	_____
A small animal	_____	Of the head	_____

Writing

Letters can be either long or short. Letters from close friends or family abroad are usually long, but letters of invitation, thanks, or apology are usually short.

 A Read the following letter carefully.

The greeting is placed on the left-hand side. Note the use of capital letters and the placing of the comma at the end of the greeting.

The date is written under the last line of the address.

The writer's full address is written at the top right-hand side of the page.

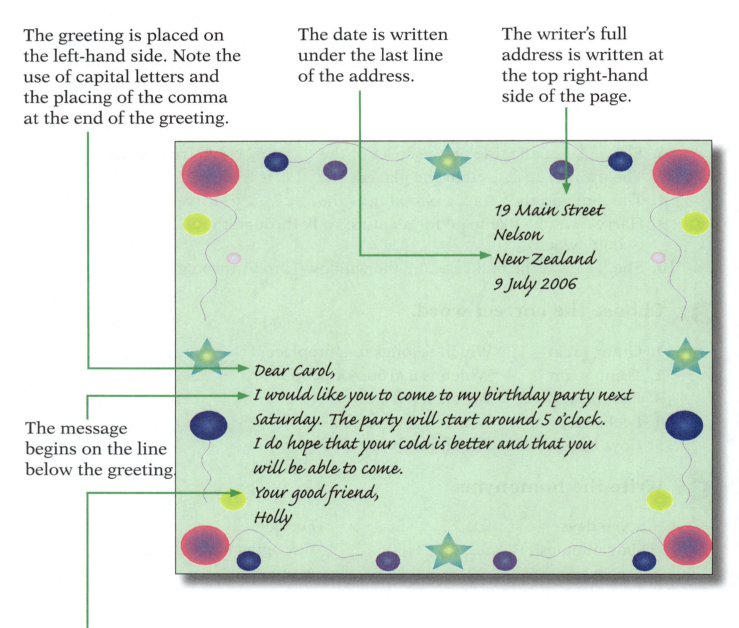

19 Main Street
Nelson
New Zealand
9 July 2006

Dear Carol,
I would like you to come to my birthday party next Saturday. The party will start around 5 o'clock. I do hope that your cold is better and that you will be able to come.
Your good friend,
Holly

The message begins on the line below the greeting.

The ending is written on the left-hand side and the writer's name is placed below it, for example:

        Your fond son,   Yours sincerely,   Best wishes,
        Yours faithfully,   Yours,   Love from,

Grammar

> A **verb** is a **doing** or **action** word – The boy **ran** quickly.

A Write the verbs.

1. House spiders weave cobwebs.
2. The squirrel built a drey.
3. The otter caught a fat moorhen.
4. The cat is purring near the fire.
5. Run before the rhino charges.
6. I shall feed the robins.
7. A monkey chatters and an ape gibbers.
8. At night the owl hoots in the forest.
9. Tom will train the horse for the big race.
10. The tiger chased the wild goat.

B Choose suitable verbs.

1. The horse _____ over the fence.
2. The fox _____ the goose.
3. A herd of buffaloes _____ across the valley.
4. The fisherman _____ a shoal of herring.
5. A frog _____ bigger than a tadpole.
6. The sly fox _____ from the hounds.
7. The angry dog _____ at the stranger.
8. A gaggle of geese _____ across the road.

C Write a verb that is opposite to the verb in Italics.

1. Dan *loved* the monkeys but Lynn _____ the elephants.
2. He *sold* his old bicycle and _____ a new one.
3. When the teacher *appeared* at the window the children _____ quickly.
4. *Shut* the door and _____ the windows.
5. I *remember* people's names but _____ their addresses.
6. The elephant *lowered* its leg and _____ its trunk.
7. We *started* the exam in the morning and _____ it in the afternoon.
8. Ann *broke* the latch on the window but she later _____ it.

Reading

 A Read the text.

Tyrannosaurus

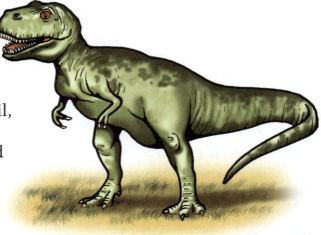

The enormous tyrannosaurus was the largest meat-eating dinosaur and was probably the most *fearsome* hunter the Earth has ever known. It grew up to fourteen metres long and up to five metres tall, and it weighed up to five tonnes. It had a powerful tail, tiny front legs, or 'arms', and a huge head. Its *massive* jaw was over a metre long and opened one metre wide.

As they were so short, the tyrannosaurus' 'arms' weren't much use for killing. Even so, dinosaur experts reckon they were still at least three times as strong as human arms.
A tyrannosaurus's main weapon was its huge mouth. Its curved, saw-like teeth were longer than a human hand and its jaw was *immensely* strong, tearing easily through its prey's bones as well as its flesh.
The tyrannosaurus had to swallow its food whole, because it couldn't chew. *Experts* have guessed that the tyrannosaurus could probably swallow up to 70 kilograms of meat in one gulp. *Fossils* show that the tyrannosaurus even fought each other – tyrannosaurus teeth marks have been found on tyrannosaurus bones.

The first tyrannosaurus skeleton to be discovered almost complete was found in Montana, in the USA, about one hundred years ago. Until then, only a few *scattered* bones had been dug up. Altogether, over twenty tyrannosaurus fossils have been found so far, but only three of these include complete skulls. The tyrannosaurus remains have been discovered in places as far apart as Canada, the USA and Mongolia, which suggests they may have lived over a fairly large part of the Earth.

Along with all the other *species* of dinosaur that were alive at the time, the tyrannosaurus became *extinct* around 65 million years ago. No one really knows why this happened, but there are two main *theories*. Some experts think the Earth's weather changed naturally, becoming gradually cooler, which meant it was eventually too cold for dinosaurs to survive. Other experts think a large meteor that crashed into the Earth at around this time caused the weather to change suddenly, with the same effect.

70

Activities

A **Answer these questions.**

1. What was the tyrannosaurus?
2. Why was the tyrannosaurus special?
3. Which part of its body was its main weapon?
4. How much meat could the tyrannosaurus swallow in one gulp?
5. How do we know the tyrannosaurus fought each other?
6. When did dinosaurs become extinct?
7. Why might dinosaurs have become extinct?
8. Which extinction theory do you prefer? Why?

B **Look up the words in *italics* in your dictionary. Write a sentence for each one.**

C **Summarise the story in your own words. Use about ten sentences.**

Phonics

Three-letter Blends

A **Unscramble these squ words.**

lerri	hsa	ear	ezee
squ _ _ _ _ _	squ _ _ _	squ _ _ _	squ _ _ _ _
di	hcel	kea	rti
squ _ _	squ _ _ _ _	squ _ _ _	squ _ _ _

B **Write the correct words.**

squeeze   square   squid   squash   squirrel   squeal   squiggle
squeak   squabble   squirt

1. The _____ is a sea creature with ten arms.
2. The elephant tried not to _____ the mouse.
3. I tried to _____ out the last of the toothpaste.
4. A _____ is a small animal with a bushy tail.
5. A silly argument is called a _____ .
6. A _____ is a shape with four sides.
7. My little sister began to _____ when I threw water at her.
8. I drew a small _____ on the chalkboard.
9. The door will _____ if it is not oiled.
10. My sister tried to _____ water at me.

Grammar

Quotation Marks

> When writing sentences, only the words that are spoken are written inside the quotation marks.
> Examples:
> 1. "I wish we could go swimming today," said Fiona.
> 2. Sahira said, "She is a fine dancer."
> 3. "Where will we leave the bicycles?" asked Maha.

A Rewrite using quotation marks, commas and question marks.

1. Paul has ruined my painting sobbed Lin.
2. Did you hear about the flood in Main Street asked Neil.
3. I sentence you to one month in prison said the judge.
4. Once upon a time there was a small cottage in the woods whispered the storyteller.
5. The huntsman roared The fox is making for the woods.
6. Khalia promised I will return your books on Friday.
7. Shin wished I hope granny brings one of her chocolate cakes.
8. I know nothing about the stolen watch lied James.
9. Do not stray from the forest path warned Little Red Riding Hood's grandmother.
10. The captain urged We must try harder in the second half.

B Rewrite using capital letters, full stops, commas and quotation marks.

yesterday pedro and isabella had great fun in the orange grove the day was sunny and warm and suitable for orange picking isabella enjoyed picking the fruit she wore gloves to save the skin of the oranges being spoilt her brother pedro climbed the ladder and picked an orange from the top of the tree just imagine isabella said pedro this orange I'm picking may be eaten by an English boy at noon their father arrived in a truck to collect the fruit he was very pleased with their work they quickly loaded the fruit on to the truck their father allowed them to travel with him to the market in madrid as they sped along the dusty road towards the big city he turned to them and said next sunday i will take the pair of you to valencia

73

Descriptive

Writing

A Write an interesting description or story about each animal. Use the help words.

Elephant

> biggest land animal   trunk   trumpets   ambles
> lives in a herd   ivory tusks   powerful

_____
_____
_____
_____

Camel

> hot Arabian desert   strong and sturdy   dried grass and grain
> beast of burden   chews dates   humped back

_____
_____
_____
_____

B Describe a trip into the desert to search for the ruins of a lost city. Use the help words.

> continued our journey   thirsty and hungry   came to an oasis*
> cool palm trees   desert fruits   a welcome rest   trudged onwards
> a great discovery   buried under sand   fallen walls   broken statues
> began to dig   precious beads   gold coins   the journey homewards
>
> * An oasis is a spot in the desert where water is found and grass and trees can grow.

Using Words

Language

 A Try this creepy crawlies crossword.

Reading

 A Read the text.

Dako

Dako, is a young *native* South American. He is a member of a tribe of Indians, called the Xingus, who live in the middle of Brazil's rainforest. Their settlement is on the banks of the River Xingu.

Dako's tribe is one of sixteen tribes who share the Xingu Park *region* of the Amazon jungle. The river gives them the regular supply of fish and fresh water they need. They also hunt wild animals that come to drink near the water's edge.

Dako's home was built by his father and members of the tribe. First, they cleared away a large patch of forest land with their axes. Then they cut down the tall trees, ferns and creepers leaving a single palm tree standing in the centre of the clearing around which they built a large bamboo frame. The frame was fastened with ropes made from creepers. Next, the cone-shaped hut was thatched and lined with large palm leaves and sheets of bark. A curtain of leaves covers a small entrance at the side of the hut. Inside the hut a fire is kept *smouldering*. The smoke helps keep beetles, flies and mosquitoes away.

Dako often goes hunting with his tribe. They use blowpipes over two metres long to shoot small animals and birds high up in the trees. A hunting trip is always exciting and dangerous. The shrieks of parrots and toucans echo through the *dense* jungle.

The Xingus are expert trackers and move with caution so as not to disturb a nest of red ants or a poisonous snake. The hunters feast on wild berries, honey and bananas.

The tribe fish in hollowed-out tree trunks and use sharp, pointed spears to *harpoon* turtles and fish. They keep a lookout for alligators that might overturn the canoe and *devour* them.

The tribesmen weave baskets and cook wild berries and cassava roots. The roots are peeled and soaked in water to remove their poison. The mashed roots are then cooked over the fire and are eaten by the tribe.

Activities

A Answer these questions.

1. Where does Dako live?
2. What is the name of his tribe?
3. Why does the tribe live near a river?
4. How was the hut built?
5. What is the purpose of the fire?
6. How are the Xingus like the Stone Age people?
7. What food do Dako and his friends eat?
8. What weapons have the Xingus?

B Look up the words in *italics* in your dictionary.
Write a sentence for each one.

C Summarise the story in your own words.
Use about ten sentences.

D Choose a word for each sentence.

> bravely   sweetly   loudly   easily   slowly   carefully   angrily   sharply

1. The warrior fought _____ .
2. The fishermen's boat moved _____ against the current.
3. Hunters must tread _____ when walking in the jungle.
4. Dako's mother sang _____ as she cooked the cassava.
5. The tree fell _____ when it was cut down.
6. Dako's father tied the roof on _____ with leaves.
7. Dako's spear stuck _____ into his prey.
8. The fishermen yelled _____ when the thief stole their fish.

E You are a photographer for a magazine.
Describe two photographs that you might take for an article about the Xingu tribe.
Draw your photographs.

Fun Time

Language

A Write the words. They all begin with the letter **A**.

1. It is the fruit of the oak. _____
2. An _____ a day keeps the doctor away.
3. A range of mountains in South America. _____
4. It is Ireland's most famous theatre. _____
5. This is a musical instrument. _____
6. It is a playing card with only one spot. _____
7. An American animal related to the crocodile. _____
8. He was a slave who wrote fables. _____
9. The air around the Earth. _____
10. A person who travels in space. _____
11. This blank book can contain stamps, photographs, etc. _____
12. A thick warm jacket. _____
13. The juice of this plant is bitter. _____
14. The second longest river in the world. _____

B Unscramble the wet weather words. Find them in the wordsearch.

brumeall _____
inartoac _____
volgse _____
rfasc _____
oranka _____
htarani _____
peac _____
eliwlntgnos _____
pac _____
tmitnes _____
fumf _____
cabalvlaa _____

w	a	b	d	e	f	g	h	s	i	j
d	e	b	r	m	u	f	f	c	c	k
u	h	l	a	a	i	n	m	a	a	l
m	o	g	l	l	i	t	q	r	p	s
b	o	l	a	i	a	n	t	f	e	u
r	d	o	w	l	n	c	c	e	x	y
e	z	v	l	c	o	g	l	o	n	m
l	n	e	o	a	p	s	t	a	a	s
l	q	s	t	p	s	t	h	o	v	t
a	n	o	r	a	k	u	v	e	n	a
w	i	r	a	i	n	h	a	t	s	s

78

Grammar

Suffixes

> When a verb ends in a **silent e**, drop the letter e before adding **ing**.
> Example: whistle, whistling.

A Add ing to these verbs.

cackle	_____	quack	_____	pine	_____
gallop	_____	bubble	_____	shine	_____
croak	_____	howl	_____	whistle	_____
search	_____	lap	_____	creak	_____
blossom	_____	crackle	_____	clank	_____
scream	_____	clatter	_____	rattle	_____
shuffle	_____	bray	_____	neigh	_____

B Write the missing word. Use the words above.

1. I saw a bird _____ for a juicy worm.
2. Mary heard the bullfrogs _____ in the pond.
3. The _____ wind whistled through the keyhole.
4. The _____ daffodils unfolded their golden bonnets.
5. The silvery grey stallion went _____ across the field.
6. The _____ stream gurgled over rocks and boulders.
7. The warm sun was _____ brightly in the clear blue sky.
8. The _____ of firewood frightened the timid squirrel.
9. The birds were _____ merrily in the hedgerows and bushes.
10. The donkey was _____ and the horse was _____ .

C Add ful to the following words and write the new words.

success	_____	harm	_____	sorrow	_____
colour	_____	care	_____	joy	_____
help	_____	peace	_____	cheer	_____
hand	_____	sin	_____	right	_____
event	_____	tear	_____	dread	_____
master	_____	mourn	_____		

Writing

A You find a magical creature at the bottom of your garden. Describe the creature's size, appearance and habits. Say where it lives and what it likes to eat.
Use the help words.

> vanished   elf   tricks   pixie   nymph   pointed ears   genie
> fairy wings   music   woodland   startled   spell-bound   charm
> magical powers   wish

_____
_____
_____
_____
_____

B Describe some clowns that you saw at the circus.
Use the help words.

> multi-coloured clothes   cherry-red noses   powdered faces
> rosy-red cheeks   baggy trousers   enormous boots   funny hats
> danced   jumped   rolled   funny antics   peals of laughter
> walked clumsily   fell awkwardly   somersaulted
> crowd laughed heartily   pie throwing

_____
_____
_____
_____
_____

Using Words

Language

A Replace said in these sentences. Use the words from the list.

| whispered | complained | shouted | asked | ordered | begged |
| reported | announced | told | advised |

1. Ali (said) _____ that the weather was terrible.
2. "Will you lend me your pencil?" (said) _____ Peter.
3. Aditi (said) _____ a secret in my ear.
4. "Please take us to the zoo," (said) _____ the children.
5. "The train is coming," (said) _____ Granddad.
6. Mary (said) _____ a story in class yesterday.
7. "Stay in bed for the rest of the week," (said) _____ the doctor.
8. The general (said) _____ that the army was to retreat.
9. The police (said) _____ to the detective that the evidence was missing.
10. The principal (said) _____ that we could have the rest of the day off.

B Replace then in these sentences. Use the words from the list.

| finally | next | later on | shortly afterwards | at last | soon |
| almost immediately | soon afterwards | after that | in a little while |

Somewhere in the hills, a tiny spring gushed out of the rock and trickled happily over smooth stones and shiny pebbles. (Then) _____, it was a dancing stream that rushed down the valley, past huge boulders and tall pine trees. (Then) _____, it was joined by another stream and (Then) _____ by another and another. (Then) _____ it became a swift flowing river that roared onwards with great power and force. (Then) _____ it passed a small village at the foot of the hills, where laughing children tossed bits of wood into its racing current. (Then) _____, it flowed under the arch of a sturdy stone bridge where a fisherman sat, his line dangling hopefully into the foaming waters. (Then) _____ it reached the flat, level land of the plain and the river then slowed down, becoming silent, dark and deep. (Then) _____ it was winding its way lazily through wide fields of rich green grass. (Then) _____ it came upon a noisy city where huge buildings and tall smoky chimneys crowded the skyline. (Then) _____ it flowed out into the sea.

Reading

 A Read the poem.

The Marrog

My desk's at the back of the class
And nobody knows
I'm a Marrog from Mars
With a body of brass
And seventeen fingers and toes.
Wouldn't they shriek if they knew
I've three eyes at the back of my head
And my hair is bright purple
My nose is deep blue
And my teeth are half yellow, half red?
My five arms are silver with knives on them
sharper than spears.
I could go back right now if I liked –
And return in a million light years.
I could gobble them all for
I'm seven feet tall
And I'm breathing green flames from my ears.
Wouldn't they yell if they knew
If they guessed that a Marrog was here?
Ha-ha they haven't a clue –
Or wouldn't they tremble with fear.
Look, look a Marrog
They'd all scream and shout.
The blackboard would fall and the ceiling
would crack
And the teacher would faint I suppose.
But I grin to myself sitting right at the back
And nobody nobody knows.

R.C. Scriven

82

Activities

A **Answer these questions.**

1. Who wrote the poem?
2. Does the poem rhyme?
3. Where is the Marrog from?
4. Do the pupils realise there's an alien at the back of the class?
5. Why don't the pupils realise there's a Marrog in class?
6. What, do you think, are the Marrog's three eyes for?
7. The Marrog is seven feet tall. What height is this in metres and centimetres?
8. Why is the Marrog grinning to himself?

B **Draw and colour a picture of the Marrog. Make sure it is exactly as it is described in the poem.**

C **Write a paragraph explaining why and how the Marrog has come to Earth. It can end with the creature sitting at the back of the class.**

D **Suddenly the Marrog made himself visible to the class. The teacher fainted … Finish the story!**

E **Can you find 12 school words in the wordsearch?**

1. _____
2. _____
3. _____
4. _____
5. _____
6. _____
7. _____
8. _____
9. _____
10. _____
11. _____
12. _____

a	b	c	d	a	r	t	k	y	e	f	g
h	i	c	g	l	o	b	e	a	j	k	l
r	m	h	n	r	u	l	e	r	o	y	p
e	q	a	r	p	s	t	u	d	p	e	s
b	v	i	w	x	e	y	z	o	p	o	l
b	k	r	s	k	a	n	c	m	a	k	h
u	s	w	g	o	b	e	l	l	k	c	u
r	e	s	a	l	i	c	n	e	p	o	s
f	d	f	b	g	b	o	o	k	v	l	s
t	e	a	c	h	e	r	g	b	i	c	l

Adverbs

Grammar

> **Adverbs** are words that tell us more about a verb.
> Most adverbs are formed by adding **ly** to adjectives.
> Example: The bird sang **sweetly**.

A Change the adjectives to adverbs.

1. He (quick) _____ swam the first length of the pool.
2. She argued (bitter) _____ with her mother.
3. The sun shone (brilliant) _____ over the crowded stadium.
4. The actress spoke (calm) _____ and (slow) _____ .
5. He won (superb) _____ .
6. She (brave) _____ rescued the drowning puppy.
7. The captain spoke (quiet) _____ to his team.
8. The police officer eyed the man (suspicious) _____ .
9. We sat (patient) _____ in the waiting room.
10. The king ruled his kingdom (wise) _____ .

> For adjectives ending in y, change the y to i and add ly.
> Example: The man was **weary**. The man walked **wearily**.

B Change the adjectives to adverbs.

1. The bored child yawned (lazy) _____ .
2. The footballer fell (heavy) _____ on his shoulder.
3. The bee works (busy) _____ from dawn to dusk.
4. The train rumbled (noisy) _____ towards the city.
5. The baby gurgled (happy) _____ in the cot.
6. The old man chuckled (merry) _____ to himself.
7. We returned to the haunted castle and entered (wary) _____ .
8. The teacher looked (angry) _____ at the pupil.
9. The level of the water rose (steady) _____ .
10. The impatient businessman left (hasty) _____ .

Writing

Adjectives

A You have just invented a marvellous machine that can take you anywhere!
Write about an adventure into the future; into the past; into space; underground or under the sea!

B One day in the playground, you found a hat. When you put it on, you became invisible!
Write a story about all the fun you had that day!

Language

Using Words

A Choose the correct word.

Goldilocks

Once upon a time (an, a) _____ little girl called Goldilocks went for a walk in the (wood, would) _____ . She did not (know, no) _____ that there were dangerous animals in the (wood, would) _____ .

Suddenly she came upon a little house.

"(I, me) _____ wonder who lives (here, hear) _____ ," she thought.

"(There, their) _____ doesn't seem to be anybody about."

She knocked on the door and walked in. In front (of, off) _____ her (were, where) _____ three bowls of steaming porridge.

She tasted the first one and screamed, "This porridge is (too, to) _____ hot (to, too) _____ eat!"

There were (two, to) _____ bowls left so she tasted another (won, one) _____ .

"Yuk! This porridge is (too, to, two) _____ sweet!" she shouted.

There (were, was) _____ one bowl left so she tasted that one.

"Mmm! This porridge is just (write, right) _____ !" she said.

Goldilocks was so tired that she fell asleep in a small bed. She did not know that the Three (Bears, Bares) _____ who lived (there, their) _____ had returned from their walk in the woods.

Father Bear shouted "Who (are, is) _____ sleeping in Baby Bear's bed?"

Mother Bear shouted, "Who (do, does) _____ she think she is?"

Goldilocks jumped up and ran away.

Baby Bear shouted after her, "Next time (bye, buy) _____ your own porridge!"

Poor Goldilocks! She (done, did) _____ not (no, know) _____ what she had (did, done) _____ wrong!

Fun Time

Language

A Write the words. They all begin with the letter **B**.

1. The capital city of Germany. _____
2. When a man lets the hair on his face grow, he grows a _____ .
3. An anchored float in the sea. _____
4. A one-storey house. _____
5. It is a flat-bottomed boat seen on canals. _____
6. It measures pressure in the atmosphere. _____
7. A large building where soldiers live. _____
8. This country grows a lot of coffee. _____
9. A horse wears it on his head. _____
10. A horse neighs. A lamb _____ .
11. It is worn round the waist. _____
12. The capital of Belgium. _____
13. It is the cutting part of the knife. _____
14. A flying mammal. _____
15. It is a large, buzzing fly. _____

B Unscramble the sports words. Find them in the wordsearch.

bootfall _____
foularm noe _____
folg _____
hicsletat _____
nisten _____
paeryl _____
emat _____
tecompe _____
chpionam _____
gloa _____

f	g	o	l	f	q	j	i	s	h
c	o	p	l	a	y	e	r	s	c
o	a	r	a	p	v	u	c	b	h
m	l	w	m	r	l	i	y	m	a
p	f	l	p	u	t	a	a	n	m
e	c	e	a	e	l	e	m	k	p
t	h	l	l	b	t	a	n	d	i
e	a	h	o	g	r	t	o	t	o
r	t	e	n	n	i	s	w	n	n
a	f	o	o	t	b	a	l	l	e

87

Reading

 A Read the text.

Everest

It wasn't until the 1930s that Mount Everest, standing on the border of Tibet and Nepal, was *officially* recognised as the highest point on Earth.

The mountain stretches so high up into the *atmosphere* that the air becomes very thin, making it impossible to breathe without an oxygen supply. It is so cold that no animals or plants can survive on its higher slopes.

By 1953, at least ten *expeditions* had set out to climb the 8848 metres to the summit of Everest, but all of them failed in the attempt. They met with fierce snowstorms, dangerous ice and bottomless *chasms*, and the lives of many brave climbers were lost.

In March of that year, another expedition was mounted to *conquer* this mighty mountain. Their plan was to set up eight camps along the way to the summit. Then two men would be chosen to make a final climb of 1000 metres to the top.

The climb was as difficult and dangerous as they expected. Slowly but surely, they edged their way upwards. When the final camp had been set up, two men left to make a last attack on the summit. Hours later, they were forced to return to camp. The weather was getting worse and there was time for only one last attempt. Edmund Hillary from New Zealand and Tenzing Norgay of Nepal were picked. With a great effort of bravery, strength and skill, they made their way onwards and upwards.

Two days later they still had not reached the summit. Once more they had to sleep in their tiny tent, only a few hundred metres from the top. A *blizzard* blew around them. They were so near and yet so far!

However, on 29 May 1953, to their delight and surprise, Hillary and Tenzing awoke to find calm and sunny weather. Later that morning they became the first people to climb the highest mountain in the world.

Activities

A Answer these questions.

1. Where is Mount Everest?
2. How high is it?
3. Give four reasons why Everest is such a difficult mountain to climb.
4. How many expeditions had failed to climb the mountain by 1953?
5. What was the plan of the next expedition?
6. Who were chosen to make the final attempts on the summit?
7. What were they delighted to see on the morning of 29 May 1953?
8. List the qualities needed to make a good mountain climber.

B Look up the words in *italics* in your dictionary.
Write a sentence for each one.

C Summarise the story in your own words.
Use about ten sentences.

D Use this table to decode the **adverbs** in the story.
Rewrite the story with the adverbs.

A	B	C	D	E	F	G	H	I	J	K	L	M
1	2	3	4	5	6	7	8	9	10	11	12	13

N	O	P	Q	R	S	T	U	V	W	X	Y	Z
14	15	16	17	18	19	20	21	22	23	24	25	26

The climber (19,12,15,23,12, 25) took off her backpack and (3,1,18, 5, 6, 21,12,12, 25) opened up the tent. She was (9, 14, 3,18, 5, 4, 9, 2, 12, 25) tired and (5, 24, 20, 18, 5, 13, 5, 12, 25) cold. The wind howled (23, 9, 12, 4, 12, 25) around her as she settled (21, 14, 3, 15,13, 6, 15, 18, 20, 1, 2, 12, 25) in her sleeping bag. Her legs were aching (2, 1, 4, 12, 25) and she was breathing (4, 5, 5, 16, 12, 25) on her oxygen. Everyone thought that she would give up (5, 1, 19, 9, 12, 25) but she was (21, 20, 20, 5, 18, 12, 25) determined to reach the summit.

Phonics

Three-letter Blends: 'shr' and 'thr'

A Unscramble the missing letters for the **thr** words.

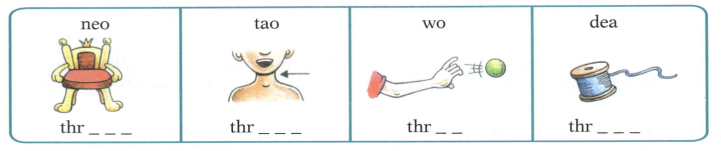

neo	tao	wo	dea
thr _ _ _	thr _ _ _	thr _ _	thr _ _ _

B Unscramble the missing letters for the **shr** words.

pim	kin	we	bu
shr _ _ _	shr _ _ _	shr _ _	shr _ _

C Write **shr** or **thr**.

1. A _____ub is a small bush which you might find in the garden.
2. When sewing a button you need a needle and _____ead.
3. The _____ush is a songbird.
4. The puppy tore the newspaper into _____eds.
5. I don't want my new top to _____ink in the wash.
6. Mandy gets a great _____ill from parachute jumping.
7. A queen sits on her _____one.
8. The little girl caught a _____imp in the rock pool.

D Find these **shr** and **thr** words in the wordsearch.

shrug   throat
shriek three
shrew   throne
shrink throb
shred   threat

l	t	h	r	o	a	t	e	t	r
g	h	h	e	l	t	h	r	o	b
n	r	u	r	t	h	r	e	a	t
k	e	l	a	w	h	o	s	o	n
o	e	e	e	s	s	n	h	i	i
e	i	r	m	g	h	e	r	w	i
a	h	f	u	o	r	u	i	s	r
s	o	r	o	y	i	n	l	e	
s	h	r	e	d	e	o	k	h	p
s	d	e	p	n	k	s	t	i	e

90

Grammar

Verbs

> **Passed is a verb.**
> Example: The bat **passed** over my head.
> **Past is a preposition or adverb** meaning by, along, beyond or after.
> Example: The tawny owl flitted **past** my window.

A Write past or passed.

1. Meera saw a colony of bats as she walked _____ the church.
2. Mina got a fright when the bat flew _____ .
3. The proud eagle swooped _____ her nest.
4. Many days _____ before my racing pigeon returned home.
5. They saw many roosting bats as they _____ through the cave.
6. The wild dog _____ on the dreaded disease, rabies.
7. At half _____ eight the bus _____ by my house.
8. It flew _____ in wide circles and _____ over the marshy swamp.
9. I _____ many happy hours watching the salmon leaping over the falls.
10. He _____ the library every day at half _____ three.

B Choose the most suitable verb for each sentence.

1. The busy bee _____ (strolled, prowled, flitted) across the room.
2. The striped beetle _____ (charged, waded, crawled) under the stone.
3. The pretty butterfly _____ (hopped, hobbled, hovered) near the rose bushes.
4. The timid snail _____ (flew, glided, scampered) along the damp grass.
5. The house spider _____ (strode, strolled, scurried) into its web.
6. The fat worm _____ (walked, waddled, wriggled) into its burrow.
7. The prickly hedgehog _____ (tickled, stung, prodded) the dog with its spines.
8. The golden eagle _____ (grabbed, tore, trapped) the lamb in its talons.
9. The croaking bullfrog _____ (leaped, limped, flew) into the deep pool.
10. The brown hen _____ (sniffed, pecked, gnawed) the pan of oats.

Writing

A Finish the story. Use the help words.

> escaped   frilly   savage   curved claws   large wings   wicked teeth
> jaws   thick   roared   rescued princess   wrinkled skin
> clumsy walk   spiked necks   dagger-sharp   hissed
> flaming nostrils   armour-plated tails   blazing eyes

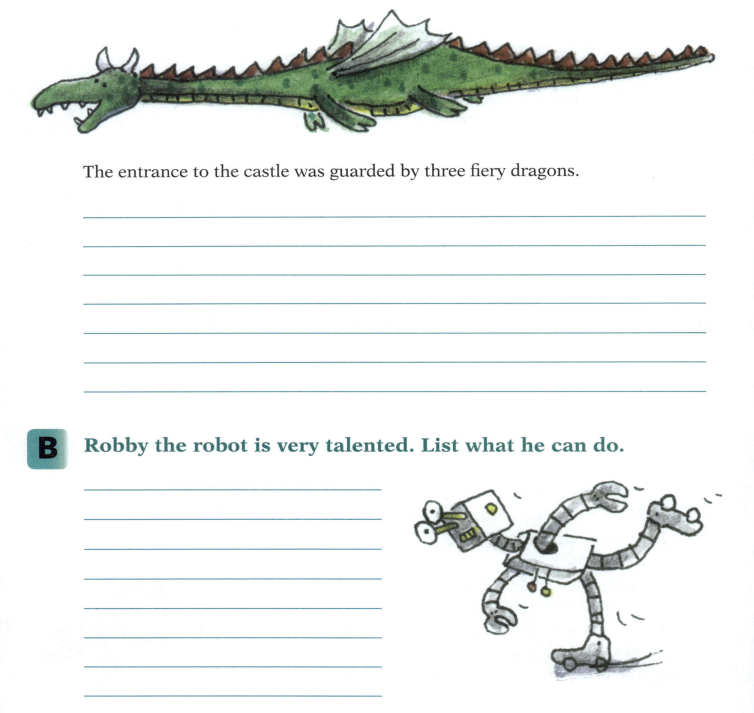

The entrance to the castle was guarded by three fiery dragons.

_____
_____
_____
_____
_____
_____
_____

B Robby the robot is very talented. List what he can do.

_____
_____
_____
_____
_____
_____
_____

Phonics

Revision

A Copy this crossword onto squared paper.

Across

2. spelled with a j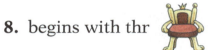
3. ends in ild
5. ir word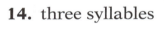
8. begins with thr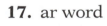
9. ur word
13. begins with shr
14. three syllables
16. silent b
17. ar word
18. four syllables

7. ends er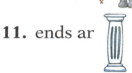
10. silent g
11. ends ar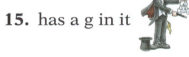
12. ends ind
13. begins with squ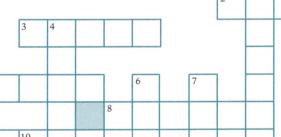
15. has a g in it

Down

1. silent t
4. or word
6. silent l

Language

A Write to, two or too.

1. Mansa blew _____ hard when learning _____ play the recorder.
2. Ann complains that she always has _____ much homework _____ do.
3. Latif is able _____ play a tune or _____ on his keyboard now.
4. _____ heads are better than one.
5. The piano was far _____ expensive _____ buy.
6. I bought _____ tickets _____ go _____ see the play.

B Write of or off.

1. Thousands _____ them floated _____ down the river.
2. The fox ran _____ with two _____ the farmer's hens.
3. Hana turned _____ the television before going _____ to bed.
4. Tim, the baby _____ family, was afraid _____ the dog next door.
5. The sphinx had the body _____ a lion and the head _____ a human.
6. The tall runner set _____ before the rest _____ the field.

C Write has or have.

1. As an art, music _____ much in common with painting.
2. The world _____ many attractive sounds.
3. We _____ to meet the composer and she _____ to meet us.
4. A minim _____ two beats and crochets _____ only one.
5. The opera singer _____ years of training.
6. Orchestras _____ many musicians who follow a conductor.

D Choose the best verb to replace went in each sentence.

| trotted | slid | scampered | scurried | trundled | skimmed |

1. The donkey and cart (went) _____ down the dusty track.
2. The water skier (went) _____ smoothly across the water's surface.
3. Hot streams of lava (went) _____ down the mountain slope.
4. The young foal (went) _____ after the mare.
5. The squirrels (went) _____ up to their drey in the trees.
6. The horse (went) _____ along beside the jockey.

Activities

A Choose the correct word.

> bee   bear   monkey   robin   mouse   snake   lion
> horse   cockerel   frog   donkey   elephant

1. The _____ hums.
2. The _____ crows.
3. The _____ trumpets.
4. The _____ brays.
5. The _____ squeaks.
6. The _____ croaks.
7. The _____ neighs.
8. The _____ chirps.
9. The _____ hisses.
10. The _____ gibbers.
11. The _____ roars.
12. The _____ growls.

B Write the missing word.

1. A _____ of angels.
2. A _____ of foxes.
3. A _____ of bees.
4. A _____ of grapes.
5. A _____ of pups.
6. A _____ of wolves.
7. An _____ of soldiers.
8. A _____ of ships.
9. A _____ of geese.
10. A _____ of sheep.
11. A _____ of mice.
12. A _____ of warriors.

C Write the missing word.

1. The sheets were clean but the _____ were dirty.
2. The tennis player seldom practised but _____ won.
3. We had enough paint for interior walls but not enough for the _____ .
4. We pinned the banner up but it fell _____ shortly after.
5. The junior teams won the cup but the _____ teams did not win anything.
6. The girl was told to be polite and not to be _____ .

D Write the missing word.

1. As blind as a _____ .
2. As graceful as a _____ .
3. As wise as an _____ .
4. As gentle as a _____ .
5. As strong as an _____ .
6. As sly as a _____ .
7. As hungry as a _____ .
8. As brave as a _____ .
9. As proud as a _____ .
10. As agile as a _____ .
11. As slow as a _____ .
12. As fierce as a _____ .

Revision

A Choose the correct word.

1. be, bee — Which is an insect? ____
2. place, plaice — Which is the flat fish? ____
3. flour, flower — Which grows in the garden? ____
4. tale, tail — Which is a story? ____
5. herd, heard — Which is a collection of animals? ____
6. beach, beech — Which is a tree? ____
7. hair, hare — Which is a wild animal? ____
8. lair, layer — Which is a fox's home? ____
9. yew, ewe, you — Which is a female sheep? ____
10. coarse, course — Which means rough? ____
11. grate, great — Which belongs to a fireplace? ____
12. teem, team — Which is a group of people? ____
13. leek, leak — Which is a vegetable? ____
14. bow, bough — Which is a branch? ____
15. heel, heal, he'll — Which is a part of your foot? ____
16. pare, pair, pear — Which means a couple? ____
17. seas, seize, sees — Which means to grasp? ____
18. scent, sent, cent — Which is a coin? ____
19. palate, pallet, palette — Which is a painter's board? ____
20. so, sow, sew — Which means to scatter? ____
21. I'll, isle, aisle — Which is an island? ____
22. rain, rein, reign — Which is part of a horse's bridle? ____
23. meet, meat, mete — Which is food? ____
24. idle, idol, idyll — Which is a false god? ____
25. for, four, fore — Which is after three? ____
26. there, their, they're — Which means belonging to them? ____
27. bean, being, been — Which can you eat? ____

96